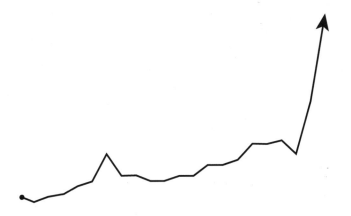

TSP Investing Strategies:

Building Wealth While
Working for Uncle Sam

By W. Lee Radcliffe

ISBN-13: 978-1461155348
ISBN-10: 1461155347
LCCN: 2011907317

This publication is designed to provide accurate and authoritative information in regard to the subject matter covered. It is sold with the understanding that neither the author nor the publisher is engaged in rendering legal, accounting, financial, or other professional service. If legal advice or other expert assistance is required, the services of a professional person should be sought.

TABLE OF CONTENTS

INTRODUCTION

I arrived at my first civilian job with the Federal Government in the summer of 2001, and the human resources office handed me a stack of papers to sign as part of my in-processing. Among the many forms that I had to fill out was a piece of paper that asked me to declare how much I wanted withdrawn from my paycheck as part of the "Thrift Savings Plan," or the TSP. At the time, this sounded to me a lot like a simple bank savings account, although I was vaguely aware that it was the Federal Government's version of a 401(k) plan. No one was available, however, to take me through the plan in detail or to provide more insight into my various investing options.

Having just finished grad school and following a cross-country relocation to the Washington, D.C. area, financially I could only afford to have a small amount deducted from each paycheck—around $50. As it was, in those first days of my Federal Government service, one entire paycheck each month went to pay rent, but I still wanted to start building up some savings after years of living the life of a poor student. The trouble was that I had never invested in any sort of stock or bond mutual funds in my life, so I had no idea how much to put where, nor how investing in the TSP fit into my other financial goals. HR had given me an 80-plus-page booklet describing the various facets of the TSP, but with all the other forms I had to fill out, I didn't have much of an opportunity to review my options in depth, and HR was not allowed to offer advice about possible TSP investing strategies. (This was before the many enhancements on TSP.gov allowing TSP investors to study the plan more thoroughly and to modify their investments online.) I chose the government bond fund, not knowing how else to begin.

As my salary slowly climbed over the next few years, I was able to increase my biweekly contributions, and my TSP account increased as well. But, as the amount in my TSP account grew, I became increasingly unsure where to put my growing savings outside of government bonds. Should I invest 100% of it in stocks? This didn't seem too wise, since the U.S. stock market had been experiencing a dramatic decline between 2000 and 2002. Or should I invest some in one fund and some in another—say, 75% in stocks and 25% in bonds, or half in stocks and half in bonds? But what if the U.S. stock market started going up? I didn't want to miss a sudden upward move in the stock market, and all the investment books I had read declared that, in the long term, stocks outperform bonds. They differed, however, on how much to invest in stocks versus bonds and what to do when stock funds were declining in value. And what about the TSP's new international and small stock funds, the I Fund and the S Fund, which had opened to investors in mid-2001? Should I invest in those funds too, and if so, how much? I was confused as to how I should allocate my investments among the five TSP funds.

I asked friends what they were doing, and I was surprised to hear the variety of answers. One said that his personal financial advisor recommended allocating 20% in each of the five funds. Another said he was investing mainly in the international and small-cap funds, hoping for rapid growth.

A third berated me for contributing at all to the bond funds, to the G Fund and the F Fund. "Why are you doing that?" he asked, bewildered. "Stocks do better than bonds. You should just invest in the stock fund." He was 100% invested in the C Fund, as were a few others I talked to. Several other coworkers did the diametric opposite, however, and invested only in government bonds, preferring the stability of the fund. One was quite excited at the amount he had saved in his first years of maxing out his TSP contributions, having saved up more than half of his first year's salary. I found myself suggesting to him that he should invest some of that in the stock fund, because "stocks do better than bonds…" But, in my gut, I wondered whether this was necessarily the case all of the time. Later, at a financial planning seminar sponsored at work, a financial advisor threw out some seemingly random percentages for allocating among the TSP investments, but even he did not explain why we should use those percentages versus any of the others.

With all these questions and after hearing the often-conflicting advice from coworkers and professional advisors, I started doing my own research. I worked hard for this money, after all, and I wanted to make sure it was working hard for me, too. I wanted to see it grow. This book is the culmination of years of research into investing in index funds such as those that are available in the TSP. I wrote this book to answer my early questions about how to invest in the TSP funds and why, and how TSP investing fits into one's overall financial goals.

In the coming chapters, I first review the basics of the Thrift Savings Plan and why it is such a good investment vehicle, relative to other investment options. I next present five strategies focused on how to diversify among the funds in the TSP for improved long-term results. In Strategy I, I pose some basic questions and hypothetical investing scenarios drawing from previous market behavior to help you determine what kind of investor you are, based on your own level of interest and risk tolerance. The next two strategies help you to establish a long-term diversification strategy for investing among the TSP funds based on your risk tolerance, and illustrate methods of re-balancing periodically without selling shares in any funds. The next strategy, Strategy IV, details how to buy into down markets for those with a higher tolerance for risk. This method is a difficult practice in the short term, but one that, over time, can yield outsized returns. This technique is not for everyone, as determined in Strategy I, but it explains how you can buy into down markets in a systematic way that will increase your returns over the long run. Strategy V explores the variety of investment vehicles available to you in addition to the TSP. By using other methods to save and invest—and pay down debt—in addition to saving and investing in the TSP, you can further diversify and expand your total investment portfolio. I also include text boxes, charts, and graphs to illustrate key points throughout the book.

I developed these strategies following several years of research and testing returns over time to improve my own TSP investing. Hearing that others had similar questions, I wrote this book to clarify the strategies so that I might share them with fellow military and Federal Government workers. I wrote this book primarily for new and mid-career military personnel and Federal Government workers who are interested in learning systematic methods of investing in the TSP but who do not know where to start. I also hope to provide a few more ideas to those who are not new to investing. While I briefly examine other life goals such as saving for a house or car, an investor's overall financial strategy will depend on personal circumstances. I am not a financial advisor by profession, and the strategies and model portfolios presented in this book might not be right for your personal situation or that of your family's, so they should be considered accordingly. As with any savings and investing plan, you should consult with those close to you and with a fee-only financial advisor as necessary to determine how investing in the TSP fits into your overall life goals.*

That said, I believe that you can successfully empower yourself to manage your own finances by doing your own research and reading to understand the basics of personal finance. You do not need overly sophisticated investment plans to build wealth over time. I believe the straightforward strategies presented below will help you to build greater wealth via the TSP and with other savings and investing methods over the long term.

I wish you success in your wealth-building efforts!

---

* Be sure to ask any financial advisor whether he or she receives any additional compensation if you put money into any of the recommended products—mutual funds, stocks, bonds, insurance, loans, etc.—presented to you. If so, that individual is *not* a fee-only advisor, but a salesman, selling you something primarily for his or her own profit!

GETTING STARTED – THE BASICS

The Thrift Savings Plan (TSP) is one of the greatest mecha-
nisms through which to build wealth in the world. Established
in April 1987, the TSP has grown to over $270 billion in as-
sets more than 20 years later. By 2010, over four million participants were contributing over $1 billion cumulatively each
month. Participants own their TSP accounts, so when they
leave government service, they can continue to access their
accounts or transfer the money into an Individual Retirement
Account (IRA) and continue to contribute to the account
each and every year thereafter to continue building wealth.

The TSP was created in the 1980s in an effort to mod-
ernize the Federal Government's retirement benefits system.
Before then, civil servants relied solely on the Civil Service
Retirement System (CSRS), the major retirement program
covering Federal civilian workers since 1920. CSRS calculated
retirement benefits based on the number of years worked: for
example, civil servants could retire with immediate benefits at
age 55 after 30 years of service or at age 60 after 20 years. But
workers in the CSRS had no access to flexible employer-sponsored, tax-deferred savings plans—sometimes called "thrift"
plans—that were growing in popularity in the private sector.

They also did not contribute to Social Security, so they were not eligible to receive Social Security for the time they worked with the government. After a lifetime of work, CSRS workers were limited to receiving a CSRS pension and nothing else.

The opportunity to work multiple careers was therefore unrealistic since Federal Government workers had to rely solely on a government pension, which in turn was based on the number of years of service as a percentage of the average of the last several years' salary.* Because they had not contributed to Social Security, former Federal Government workers—if they chose to work somewhere else—would have to start contributing to Social Security relatively late in their careers, and any pension at their new employer would be smaller, based on fewer years' service. They would also start investing in the private "thrift" plan or 401(k) sponsored by their new employer relatively late in life, limiting potential investment growth over time.

Thus, turnover in the Federal Government at the time was almost nonexistent. As Judith Havemann of *The Washington Post* noted weeks after the TSP and new retirement system were introduced, while the Federal Government experienced a 40% turnover rate among those in their first five years of service, there was "very little mobility in government" once a worker chose to make government service a career. The old retirement system "tied some workers to hated or dead-end jobs with 'golden handcuffs.'"[1]

The inflexible system, moreover, was not conducive to recruiting experienced workers to the various levels of civil service, as pensions were based primarily on the number of years served. Thus, those who began a civil service career

---

* The CSRS pension formula is a complex one that averages out to just under 2% per year of service over a career: CSRS workers with 30 years of service would receive 56.25% of the average of their highest three years' base salary as a yearly pension, for example.

in their 40s or 50s would face a smaller pension than those who began Federal Government service in their early 20s.

To help rectify these limitations while at the same time modernizing the Federal Government retirement system, on June 6, 1986, President Ronald Reagan signed legislation creating the new Federal Employee Retirement System (FERS), in which the TSP was a major new component.

While FERS reduced the percentage used to calculate a worker's pension almost in half compared to the old CSRS, FERS employees were eligible to participate in the newly created TSP, which began collecting contributions in April 1987. FERS participants could contribute up to 10% of their salaries to the TSP and enjoy tax-deferred growth, and they were eligible to withdraw the money after they turned 59½. In return for a reduced pension, they would receive up to a 5% government match on contributions to the TSP. This same basic benefit continues to this day, although the overall contribution limits have risen significantly.

After President Reagan signed the legislation creating FERS and the TSP, all civil servants hired after January 1, 1984—around 588,000 by the time President Reagan signed the legislation—were automatically transferred to the new FERS system, while the approximately two million remaining workers had until the end of 1987 to decide whether to switch. Those who chose not to switch could still take advantage of tax-deferred growth in the TSP by contributing up to 5% of their base pay to the TSP, although they did not receive matching contributions.

In its first year, the TSP had only one investment option: government bonds in the G Fund. The fund returned an annualized 8.75% in its first few months (a very generous rate compared to the 3-4% annual returns in the G Fund over 20 years later). In January of the following year, the TSP opened two new funds, the F Fund—a bond index fund—and the

C Fund that mirrored the S&P 500 index of stocks of large- and mid-sized companies in the United States. By late 1988, accounts within the TSP were worth close to $2.5 billion, and they were growing at an average of $5 million per day.[2]

The TSP has expanded and improved greatly in the 20-plus years since it was established. The total value of TSP accounts surpassed $100 billion for the first time in mid-2000. On October 30, 2000, legislation was enacted that allowed over two million members of the U.S. uniformed services to open TSP accounts the following year. Two more fund options—the I Fund international equities index fund and the S Fund small-capitalization index fund—were added to the TSP in May 2001. In 2005, a series of "Lifecycle" L Funds was established that automatically adjusts investments based on the target year of the L Fund. And contribution limits were gradually increased after 2002, with percentage limits eliminated in 2006 in favor of an upper contribution limit of $15,000, adjusted upward periodically based on inflation. From 2003, the TSP website began to provide daily closing values of each fund and to allow online interfund transfer requests. (The TSP until then allowed only one interfund transfer at the end of each month based on transfer requests received by the 15th of that month.) With these changes, the TSP has become much more transparent and flexible, allowing TSP participants greater control over their investments.

THE FUNDS

According to fund information available on the Thrift Savings Plan website (www.tsp.gov/investmentfunds/ investmentFunds.shtml), as of the end of 2009 the six types of funds featured the following characteristics:

G Fund The fund invests in short-term U.S. Treasury securities specially issued to the TSP, and the U.S. Government guarantees payment of principal and interest. Thus, it is the safest of the funds as there is no "risk of loss of principal," according to the fund information. It has returned 6.15% annually between April 1987 and December 31, 2009.* While this has "outpaced inflation and 90-day T-bills," per the TSP website, this is the lowest return among the TSP funds over this 22-year time period.

F Fund The fund is invested in the U.S. Debt Index Fund. This is an index of fixed-income securities (bonds) with maturities of over one year, comprising Treasury and Agency bonds, asset-backed securities, and corporate and non-corporate bonds. It has returned 7.1% annually between January 1988 and December 31, 2009.*

C Fund The fund invests in the largest 500 publicly traded companies in the United States, as determined by Standard and Poor's 500 (S&P 500) index. At the end of 2009, the top five companies in the C Fund included Exxon Mobil, Microsoft, Apple, Johnson & Johnson, and Procter & Gamble. Between January 1988 and December 31, 2009, the fund returned 9.55% annually.*

I Fund The only international fund in the TSP, this fund invests in all the companies listed in the Europe, Australasia, Far East (EAFE) Index of publicly traded companies in developed countries outside the

United States and Canada. The five largest companies in the I Fund at the end of 2009 were HSBC Holdings, BP PLC, Nestle, Total, and Banco Santander. This fund has a shorter history than the G, C, and F Funds, returning 4.03% annually since it opened in May 2001 through December 31, 2009.*

S Fund The fund invests in domestic U.S. companies that are not listed in the S&P 500 (C Fund) index. It invests in small- and medium-sized companies that make up the Dow Jones U.S. Completion Total Stock Market Index. Like the I Fund, the S Fund opened in May 2001, and it has returned 4.86% annually through December 31, 2009.* The largest five holdings of the S Fund at the end of 2009 were Berkshire Hathaway, Marvell Technology Group, BlackRock, Crown Castle Intl., and Annaly Capital Management.

L Funds The L Funds or "Lifecycle Funds" opened on August 1, 2005. As of the end of 2009, there are five L Funds: the L 2040, L 2030, L 2020, L 2010, and L Income funds. Each L Fund comprises a mix of the G, F, C, I, and S stock and bond funds listed above, and they slowly sell the more-volatile stock funds (the C, I, and S funds) as the funds' target dates near and invest more in the bond funds (the G and F funds) to protect investors from the ups and downs of the market and to provide more yield.*

*Note: Past performance does not mean this fund will grow the same in the future. The fund may enjoy a greater growth rate in the future, or it may go down in value as well.

As it has grown and improved over the years, the '. and its investors have enjoyed significant praise. In 198. Mike Causey, who covered Federal Government-related issues for *The Washington Post*, called the new TSP "Uncle Sam's...super-version" of the private sector's "tax-deferred 401(k) plans."[3] In 2005, Tim Middleton, a personal finance columnist for the online "MSN Money," called the TSP "possibly the finest 401(k)-style plan in the nation." According to Middleton, "federal employees who participate have proved themselves to be competent and conservative long-term investors" and "are beating the pants off of Social Security's investment performance with no more risk than displayed by private pensions in general."[4]

According to a 2006-2007 survey of TSP participants, 85% of respondents were satisfied with the plan, compared with 68% of private sector 401(k) participants who were satisfied with their plans. As a sign of TSP participants' satisfaction, those surveyed contributed an average of 10.2% of their salary to their accounts, compared with an average of 7.3% contribution among 401(k) participants in 2005. Indeed, one in ten TSP participants in the military contributed 20% of their salary despite not receiving a government contribution, indicating a high degree of commitment to saving for the future.[5]

The TSP was cited as one possible model when the Clinton and George W. Bush administrations considered the possibility of creating individual accounts as part of, or in addition to, Social Security benefits. The President's Commission to Strengthen Social Security, which issued its final report in July 2001, referred to the "Thrift Savings Plan" and TSP accounts no fewer than 16 times. The commission cited a Spring 1999 Treasury Department-contracted report declaring that the "task" of creating personal accounts "was feasible" as "Thrift Savings Accounts were already in place" and "the cost [is] modest."[6]

tion to create personal Social Security ac-
, the TSP was floated in Congress several
ᴜiting the negative savings rate in the United
, Senator Jeff Sessions proposed the creation of per-
ᴜonal savings accounts "modeled on the successful Thrift
Savings Plan for federal employees" in late 2006. "Over the
past two decades," Senator Sessions wrote in an op-ed in
The Washington Post, the TSP "has been an unqualified success, as federal employees have received large returns on the
money they invested."[7] (Social Security reform and Sessions'
proposed legislation were not passed into law, however.)

Most importantly, the TSP is quite possibly the cheapest investment vehicle in the world, especially compared to
many plans used by private employers. Christian Weller and
Shana Jenkins, writing in *Financial Planning*, lamented the
exceptionally large fees in many 401(k) plans in contrast to
the TSP. Citing a 2004 Congressional Budget Office study,
typical private-sector 401(k) fees were "between 1% and
1.5% of assets"—an astonishingly high figure—which "can
result in a *24% to a 38% reduction* in overall savings at the
end of a 40-year career" (my emphasis added). In contrast,
by 2007, TSP fees had fallen to below 0.02% of assets—in
some cases one-thirtieth those in regular 401(k) plans! As
Weller and Jenkins correctly asserted, "[s]eemingly small
annual fees cut into the compound rate of return, thus
diminishing investors' ability to build their nest eggs."[8]

The TSP does not charge any up-front fees for investing
in any of the funds, and all the funds charge very minimal expense ratios, or very small percentages each year to help pay
for services such as support staff, the TSP website, and periodic
correspondence with participants. And these expenses have
fallen considerably in the past 20 years. In 2008, the expense
ratio for each of the funds was a minuscule .018%, or a mere
$0.18 for each $1,000 invested in the stock and bond funds.

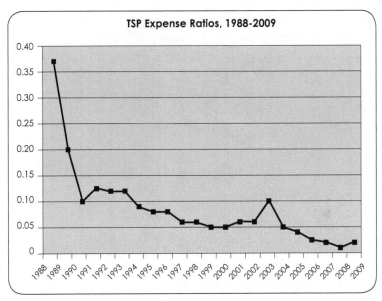

The TSP's expense ratios have dropped dramatically since it was
first established in 1987 (source: TSP website).

In contrast, the lowest expense ratio for a publicly traded index fund, the S&P 500 index Exchange Traded Fund (also called the "SPDR" ETF)—which trades much like a stock and is available through any brokerage account—is 0.07%, or $0.70 for each $1,000 invested. Both Fidelity and Vanguard offer mutual funds that track the S&P 500 index and that have expense ratios of 0.09% and 0.15%* respectively as of mid-2008. These are still very low, but a surprisingly large number of index funds have expense ratios of half a percent (0.50%) or more; the Lipper average for large-cap stock funds is 0.6%. With a 0.6% expense ratio, the fund is collecting $6 per year for every $1,000 invested, compared to $0.18 for each $1,000 in the TSP funds—almost 40 times

---

* Vanguard offers "Admiral Shares" with a .07% expense ratio for long-term account owners who meet certain account minimums.

the amount charged in the TSP. And this is in addition to any other fees the fund may charge for the privilege of investing your hard-earned money into their mutual funds.

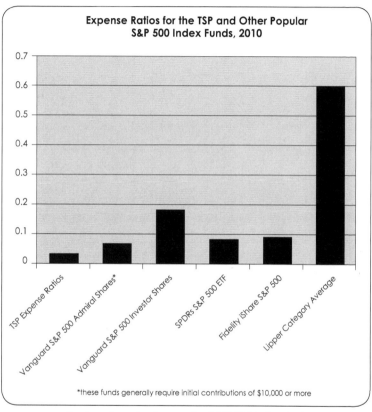

Compared to other inexpensive S&P 500 index funds, the TSP expense ratios are extremely low.

Over time, these expenses can have a major impact on the growth of your funds. To illustrate this, let's say that after diligently saving and investing for many years you have a portfolio worth $500,000 in stock and bond funds. With the TSP's extremely low 0.018% expense ratio, the TSP would collect $90 each year from your account to cover administrative expenses. If your $500,000 portfolio were instead invested in mutual funds charging a higher 0.6% expense ratio, you would instead pay $3,000 each and every year. That's a difference of $2,910 each year—meaning you would keep that extra $2,910 in your TSP fund, compared with mutual funds that charge greater expense ratios. And that difference grows as your account grows: a $1,000,000 portfolio would be charged $180 in the TSP but $6,000 in the high-expense mutual fund. Thus, the less money the fund takes from you in expenses, the more you keep, and the more money that will continue to grow for you in your TSP account in the future.

Even one of the wealthiest men in the world, Berkshire Hathaway Chairman Warren Buffett, has repeatedly highlighted the detrimental effect of expenses. In his 2004 annual letter to Berkshire shareholders, he wrote, "Investors should remember that...expenses are their enemies." Buffett attributed "investment management" fees as one of the three primary causes for investor underperformance in the past. (The other two were investing "based on tips and fads" and a "start-and-stop approach to the market marked by untimely entries...and exits" into and out of the market).[9]

In his 2006 shareholder letter, Buffett discussed more fully the relatively high fees that hedge funds charge private investors.* Private hedge funds are notorious for their high fee structure, as many hedge funds charge a 1.5% or 2% management fee each year and typically keep 20% of any gain in the funds, so that investors get only 80% of the gains of their investments (but investors of course fully

---

* Hedge funds are lightly regulated and privately run funds that can make a wide variety of investments in addition to the buying and selling of stocks, to include buying and selling commodities, commercial real estate and debt, and foreign currencies. They can also "short" these investments— bet that they will go down—as a means to "hedge" or protect their other investments (hence the name for this type of investment fund).

suffer all the losses). Buffett illustrated how detrimental this high fee structure is to an investor. "[A] manager who achieves a gross return of 10% in a year will keep 3.6 percentage points—two points off the top, plus 20% of the residual 8 points—leaving only 6.4 percentage points for his investors...He will receive this bonanza even though an index fund might have returned 15% to investors in the same period and charged them only a token fee."[10]

In fact, Buffett is so sure that fees are a drag on a stock fund's performance that he declared at the May 2006 Berkshire Hathaway annual meeting that he would bet anyone $1 million that the S&P 500 index fund would beat a basket of any ten hedge funds over a ten-year period, after their fees were included. According to *Fortune Magazine*'s Carol Loomis, a friend of Buffett and the former editor of his company's annual report, a year later the owner of a high-fee private money management firm negotiated a bet with Buffett pitting a basket of five managed hedge funds against Buffett's choice of the Vanguard S&P 500 Admiral shares fund, with an expense ratio of just .07%. With the bet officially beginning on January 1, 2008, they each put up $320,000 in a zero-coupon bond that would mature in ten years and be worth $1 million. The winner of the bet would give the money to the charity of his choice.[11] Regardless of the outcome of this particular bet, one of the most successful investors in the world demonstrated significant confidence in investing in the S&P 500—the C Fund in the TSP—over the long run, so individual investors should be confident in putting at least a portion of their long-term savings in this index fund as well.

For any investment, your goal is to keep as much money as you can in your account so your investments continue to grow, and the lower the expenses and fees, the more money you can keep for long-term growth. So to build wealth you should pay close attention to minimizing expenses, and ultimately the TSP offers the lowest expenses in the business.

So how is the TSP able to keep expenses so low? One of the main reasons is because the funds invest passively in bonds and stocks according to broad indexes. The indexes list the company stocks and government and company bonds from largest to smallest in size, and fund managers purchase the stocks and bonds according to this list. The TSP funds thus go up and down as the broad stock and bond markets go up and down. Because there is no guessing involved as to which companies will do better than others—investors in these funds own them all according to size—the index funds perform just as well as (or just as poorly as) the broad markets. These funds do not buy or sell stocks or bonds very often, and this saves TSP investors money since each trade requires the payment of a commission to buy or sell a stock or bond. And because the TSP manages several hundred billion dollars in the five funds, the TSP enjoys significant economies of scale.

How is the "stock market" different from an "index fund" and the TSP funds?

The **stock market** is the collection of all stocks traded in a specific country. In the United States, stocks are traded—bought and sold—on two major **stock exchanges**: the New York Stock Exchange (NYSE) and the Nasdaq (the acronym for the rather arcane "National Association of Securities Dealers Automated Quotation," which is no longer used). The NYSE is the older of the two, with origins dating to 1792. The Nasdaq began as the first all-electronic stock exchange in 1971, and because of its early tech-friendly image, it attracted more technology companies in its early years. One general way to know whether a company is listed on the NYSE or on the Nasdaq is to look at a company's ticker symbol: if it has one, two, or three letters, it is most likely listed on the NYSE, but if it has four letters, it is probably listed on the Nasdaq. Thus, "General Electric" is listed on the NYSE as "GE," and Microsoft is traded on the Nasdaq as "MSFT." Both of these exchanges are located in New York.

The S&P 500 index—which is what the **C Fund** is based on—is a list of the 500 largest U.S. companies from the largest to the 500th in market value. (The companies at the bottom of the list are not based strictly on capitalization, because company sizes can grow or contract quickly depending on how many investors are buying or selling their stock.) These companies are bought and sold on either the NYSE or the Nasdaq, and the C Fund buys shares of these companies on either exchange when you invest money in the C Fund. It similarly sells shares of these companies on the exchange when investors take money out of the C Fund. The **S Fund** is made up of the smaller U.S. companies from the 501st in size to about the 5000th smallest company traded in the U.S. (Because new companies are constantly being created and "going public"—selling their shares to the public for the first time—the exact number of companies on the "Dow Jones U.S. Completion" index is consistently changing.) These smaller companies can also be bought and sold on the NYSE or Nasdaq. If you invest in both the C Fund and the S Fund, congratulations! You have invested in the entire U.S. stock market.

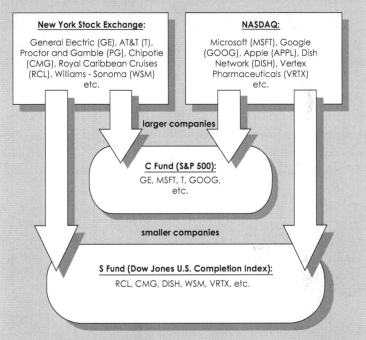

Outside the United States, there are major **stock exchanges** in places like London, Frankfurt, Tokyo, and Seoul, and non-U.S. companies are bought and sold on these various exchanges. Since the **I Fund** invests in the major non-U.S. companies found on these foreign exchanges, if you invest in the I Fund in addition to the C and S funds, you are investing in foreign stock markets, as well.

Because there is no one person or team of people trying to guess what company or companies will do better than others to improve results, the TSP does not have to pay what can be very high salaries for investment advisers, and this saves TSP investors lots of money. Investing experts charge significantly for their research and staff, even though studies show that over the long term, a majority of active money managers actually perform worse than passive index funds such as those found in the TSP. According to Burton Malkiel, an economist at Princeton University who has written extensively on the stock markets, index funds have beaten active managers by almost 2% on average each year over long periods. The poorer returns of actively managed funds are due to investment fees to pay for staff and advertising, for example, and costs associated with increased buying and selling of stocks compared to index funds, according to Malkiel.[12] Even if a money manager can beat the market by one or two percentage points each year, the fees he or she charges investors for services rendered, coupled with trading fees, actually create a *loss* on average for the individual investor over the long term.

According to Kenneth French, an academic at Dartmouth, many individual investors are simply "unaware that the average active investor would increase his return if he switched to a passive strategy"—that is, to index funds. French calculated the total cost of trying to beat the market at around .67% of a portfolio each year. Why don't more individual investors use index funds? "Financial firms certainly contribute to this confusion," according to French, and "[a]lthough a few occasionally promote index funds as a better alternative, the general message from Wall Street is that active investing is easy and profitable."[13] In other words, actively managing other peoples' money is a lucrative business because of the fees companies can collect. But in reality, the small investor quite often experiences a smaller return than what he or she would have enjoyed by investing in index funds.

It is true that over a one- or five-year period or even longer, some professional money managers do indeed beat the stock market, and they get a lot of media attention for their impressive performance over these relatively short periods of time. But almost none can do so over several decades or longer. Moreover, the odds of an investor choosing from one of the thousands of underperforming professional money managers are much, much greater than choosing the one or two who might actually be able to beat the market (or any index fund) over several decades. As *The Wall Street Journal*'s personal finance columnist Jonathan Clements wrote, "[I]f you buy index funds, you don't have to worry about badly lagging behind the market averages because you or your fund managers pick the wrong stocks."[14] Decades of research shows that index funds beat a large majority of so-called investment experts over extended periods of time, so investing in the TSP's index funds is indeed a winning strategy over time.

Additionally, many (but not all) TSP participants receive a match from the government of up to 5% of their contributions, to make up for a lower pension calculation. If you're eligible and contribute 5% of your $50,000 annual salary (only $96 every two weeks) into your TSP account, for example, the government will add an additional $96 per pay period. This *doubles* the money going into your account for the year from $2,500 to $5,000.

The match is currently reserved for members of FERS, which now constitutes the largest segment of the Federal Government civilian workforce. Thus, not all TSP participants receive a match. Uniformed personnel and civilian employees in the CSRS do not get a match, because they instead get a larger pension after working a full career with the U.S. Government. Even without the match, however, military personnel and CSRS workers can still take advantage of the rock-bottom expense ratios for the TSP index funds, as well as the tax-deferred status of the contributions until they are withdrawn, by contributing money to their individual TSP accounts.

Uniformed personnel do get a perk that civilians do not get: they can invest their special pay, incentive pay, and bonuses in the TSP. And uniformed personnel might one day receive a match too, since the secretary of each military service can decide whether to allow matching contributions for uniformed personnel who agree to serve longer terms in the military. (Cash bonuses were initially viewed as a more popular incentive, which is why the services did not match TSP contributions from 2001.) For example, the Department of the Army established a pilot program to see whether TSP matching contributions would help recruiting efforts. In this special program, those who enlisted in certain MOSs ("Military Occupational Specialties," the various job classifications in this branch of service) before September 30, 2006 were eligible to receive matches to their TSP contributions up to the first 5%.[15] While this was still a pilot program as of this writing and no decision had been made to expand the program, those serving in the military should stay tuned, as you too might one day be eligible to receive matching contributions.

If, as a FERS employee, you *don't* add any money to your TSP account, the government will only add the equivalent of 1% of your pay into the low-return government bond fund. You lose the other 4% government match, because you are not contributing to your own account. Thereafter, you receive a match based on how much you contribute up to 5% of your salary. If you contribute even 1% of your own pay to your TSP account, you get an additional

1% match from the government on top of the original 1% government contribution, for a total of 3% of your salary. Contribute 2% of your own money, and the government will throw in the original one percent plus 2% to match your contribution, for a total of 5%. (See chart below.)

If the FERS employee contributes…	the government will add…	for a total contribution of…
nothing	1%	1%
1%	2%	3%
2%	3%	5%
3%	4%	7%
4%	4.5%	8.5%
5%	5%	10%
6%	5%	11%
7%	5%	12%
8%	5%	13%
9%	5%	14%
10%	5%	15%

And as the chart above illustrates, FERS employees are not limited to contributing 5% of their salaries. They can contribute 10% or more of their salaries and still receive the 5% match, as long as the total amount including the match does not exceed $16,500 in the entire calendar year as of 2011. (This maximum amount will be increased periodically over time to match inflation.) Also, the TSP allows those aged 50 and over to make what are called "catch-up contributions" of up to $5,500 (in 2011, subject to periodic cost-of-living increases), in addition to the $16,500, for a total of $22,000. And since your contributions and the match are deposited directly to your TSP account, the entire amount is exempt from all taxes until you withdraw it any time after you turn 59½.*

As you well know, taxes can take a significant amount out of your biweekly pay, leaving you with substantially less to save. Depending on how much you make and whether you have deductions for a home mortgage, children, etc., federal and state taxes as well as deductions for Social Security and Medicare can take anywhere from one-fifth to one-third of your pay, meaning you might bring home no more than $0.67 to $0.80 for each $1 you earn after taxes are taken out. And you haven't even paid your bills yet, much less saved anything! If you save or invest some of that after-tax $0.67 to $0.80 in a taxable account, the interest on *that* money is also taxable each and every year, so you keep getting taxed again and again, year after year.

The TSP helps you avoid this. Money you contribute to your TSP account is contributed *before taxes* and before other deductions are taken out of your pay, so each $1 you earn and contribute to the TSP is a full $1 you keep for long-term growth. And, if you are eligible for the match up to 5%, that $1 becomes $2. Moreover, this $1—or $50 or $100 or $500 depending on how much you contribute each pay-day—will grow without any taxes being taken out in any of those years that it is growing and collecting interest and dividends. Only many years later when you withdraw money from the TSP is the money taxed (but *not* the remaining money in the TSP). Thus, you can choose to try to save and

---

* You may withdraw TSP funds sooner, but the withdrawn amount will under most circumstances be subject to taxes and an additional 10% early withdrawal penalty—a big hit and something to avoid at all costs. You can also take out a "loan" and pay it back over time, but this means you miss out on any growth that your investments might have enjoyed, after you took it out as a "loan," and you generally have to pay back the entire loan immediately if you leave your job.

invest some of that $0.67 to $0.80 for every $1 you earn after taxes, or you can keep up to $2 by contributing to the TSP.

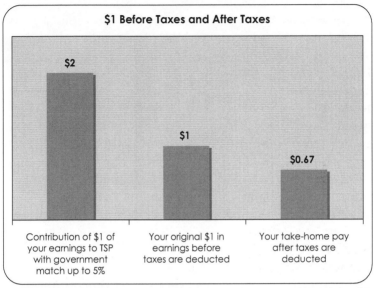

$1 Before Taxes and After Taxes

- **$2** — Contribution of $1 of your earnings to TSP with government match up to 5%
- **$1** — Your original $1 in earnings before taxes are deducted
- **$0.67** — Your take-home pay after taxes are deducted

With the government match of up to 5% of your salary, you could put up to $2 into your TSP account for every $1 you earn, but that $1 in earnings drops to between 67¢ to 80¢ after federal and state taxes are deducted. Even without a government match, you can still save a full $1 in the TSP versus taking 67¢ home, after you pay taxes.

Your periodic contributions, any government match, the TSP's extremely low fees, and the tax-deferred nature of the TSP all mean that your TSP account can grow substantially over time. And your contributions themselves can grow over the years, as you are promoted from time to time.

Here's a basic illustration. Let's say you're just starting your first Federal Government job. You're in your mid-20s and start at GS-8, Step 1. Let's say you decide to contribute 5% of your salary to the TSP, which is enough to get a full match to double the amount that goes into your personal account. If you work hard during your government service and receive periodic promotions in addition to periodic step increases, your contributions will grow as a natural result of growth in your yearly pay.

Now, let's say you invest that amount into the large-cap C stock index fund, with holdings in well-known, large, and successful U.S. companies such as Apple, Google, Procter & Gamble, and Johnson & Johnson. If the fund continues to grow at the historic market average of just over 10% per year—its average from 1926 to 2006, according to Jeremy Siegel's *Stocks for the Long Run*[16]—your contributions will grow from $0 upon starting your first week of work to $1,331,000 after a 30-year career, based on a 2008 starting salary in the Washington, D.C. metro area. This assumes a 5% increase in your base pay each year that will automatically increase your TSP contributions and the government match by a similar amount.

Depending on how you progress in your career, that 5% average yearly increase might actually be a conservative figure with additional promotions. Nevertheless, if the market performs as it has historically, and you continue to contribute to the TSP throughout your career, you could retire a millionaire, and this is in addition to receiving a basic pension for Federal Government service.

What if you contributed 10% of your salary instead of 5% over this same 30-year period? Under the same scenario, your investment would grow to $1,996,000 in 30 years—almost two million dollars for a total investment of only $289,000 (plus $144,000 in matching contributions) over that time period.

But, even if your pay were to remain at the same pay grade, your pay would still be periodically adjusted for inflation. While this might mean only 2% or 3% a year, over time, this increase can be substantial.* Let's say you remain

---

* Yearly raises to adjust for inflation are not automatic, however: illustrating how a struggling economy can impact the pay of the federal workforce, federal pay was frozen in 2011 and 2012 due to significant budget constraints.

a GS-12, Step 5, for the rest of your career. As illustrated in the graph below, the GS-12, Step 5 level worker would have received a base salary of $45,670 in 1993. By 2008, that same worker would earn $65,405 per year in base salary, a rise of almost 45% (see below). Similarly, uniformed service members enjoyed periodic increases as well, with the base pay of an E-6 with ten years' experience increasing from $1,623 in 1993 to $2,930.40 in 2008. (Private sector pay increased over this period as well.) And while some civilian departments and agencies are considering a transition from the antiquated GS scale to more flexible performance-based pay systems, salaries will most likely continue to be adjusted for inflation from time to time in a similar manner.

The base salary for a GS-12, Step 5, worker rose steadily between 1993 and 2008. As your salary increases, so too will your TSP contributions.

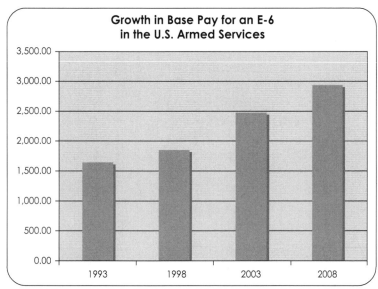

Similarly, the base pay for an E-6 in the U.S. military rose steadily between 1993 and 2008. Remember, even as your salary rises over time, you can increase your TSP contribution percentage to enjoy even faster growth in your TSP account.

But a couple of *big* caveats are needed here. First, the above calculations were based on assumptions taken from very long periods of stock market performance over many decades. The market sometimes can perform quite badly over an extended period of time, even over several years or longer. There can be periods of significant and extended market declines, with some declines of 20%, 30%, even 40% or more. Sometimes, the markets recover quite rapidly, but at other times, they take many years to recover. The value of TSP accounts invested in the F, C, S, and I funds *will* decline as the markets decline. These can be times of great opportunity, as we will see in later chapters, but they can seem very painful for those who are not mentally and emotionally prepared for the declines.

Moreover, the returns noted above were not adjusted for inflation over time, so the actual return—after taking into account the growth in prices over time of everything from food, fuel and clothes, rent and the price of a new car—would be less than the final calculations suggest.

Market risks and the risk of inflation are therefore huge challenges in constructing a TSP portfolio that will provide meaningful returns over time. Let's look at these risks more fully before moving on to the five strategies in this book.

The Risks of Saving and Investing – and of *Not* Saving and Investing

Investing in anything is inherently risky. If you invest too conservatively, your investments might not keep up with inflation. If you invest in more volatile stock funds, you might experience sudden, prolonged declines in the stock markets. But in my opinion, the risk of *not saving or not investing* any of your hard-earned money is greater than either of those risks because, if you don't save and invest, you cannot build wealth over time.

Inflation – One of the first major risks investors face over time is inflation. To illustrate the effects of inflation, let's take the above scenario as a new GS-8 employee contributing 5% salary, with the 5% match. Over a 30-year career, during which time you would have enjoyed the long-term average return of 10%, you'd end up with $1,331,000 in your TSP account. But over a 30-year time span, the prices of almost everything rise. Food and clothing become more expensive. Cars become more expensive, and rent becomes more costly, as well. Even younger employees new to the work force have gotten a taste of inflation as the price of gas and food have increased rapidly just in the past few years.

Annual inflation averaged over 3% in the 1900s. The adjusted average return of an S&P 500 index fund over 30 years, taking into consideration 3.5%+ yearly inflation, would drop from just over 10% to approximately 6.5%. Thus, instead of $1,331,000 in the TSP, you would expect to have around $709,000 in the TSP, based on higher average prices 30 years from now. A dollar today will buy less tomorrow, because prices of common goods and services will continue to increase over time. While the *actual* amount in your TSP account might still be just over $1.3 million, after 30 years of inflation, it will *feel* like $709,000 because that $1.3 million will buy less in the future than it will today. And after contributing 10% of your salary to the TSP, the amount 30 years from now would be approximately $1,064,000, adjusted for inflation, instead of just under $2 million.

While these are still significant amounts, they are close to half the original unadjusted figures and a drastic drop due to just 3.5% inflation per year. Moreover, inflation could be even worse in the future, and prices could grow by 4% or 5% or more a year. Indeed, by the end of the 1970s and into the early 1980s, inflation grew by 10% or more in some years. With 10% inflation, prices of many things would *double* in just over seven years—a $20,000 car, for example, would cost close to $40,000 in seven years at 10% yearly inflation. While we will hopefully never experience inflation on this scale again, inflation of some sort is almost always present, and rapid inflation could wreak havoc on all of our investments inside and outside the TSP. Even the "safest" of the TSP funds, the G Fund, might not be able to keep up with rapid inflation, based on returns of around 3-4% over the past few years.

Higher inflation, moreover, can cause stock prices to drop in the short term. This is because the yield on bonds—that is, the interest rate that bonds pay to investors each year—goes up as inflation goes up. The higher bond yields mean that investors can get a better interest rate in bonds in the short term than from stock dividends, and some investors will sell their stocks and invest that money in bonds to get better yields. This happened in the inflationary 1970s as bond yields rose to over 10% by the end of the decade, so people invested in bonds that had higher yields and greater perceived safety than stocks.

Over the long term, however, stocks can better adjust to inflation because companies can improve productivity to lower costs, and they can raise prices of what they charge for their goods and services, so that their earnings can recover and increase over time. And as inflation began to fall gradually from the mid-1980s, for example, investors enjoyed better returns in stocks rather than bonds over the next 18 years.

Ultimately, a well-diversified portfolio coupled with consistent additions to investments can help guard against the threat of inflation over the long term.

Declines in the Markets – TSP investors also face the risk of sometimes sudden drops in the value of markets. While market declines can occur at any time—even during generally excellent economic conditions—some declines are more dramatic than others. They are sometimes followed by long periods of stagnation, when stock markets go for many years without increasing at all. In the United States, these periods include the Depression- and WWII-eras of 1929-1949, the extended period of "stagflation" (stagnation and inflation) of 1966-1982, and the post-Internet and post-real estate bubbles of 2000 to the present. Take the late 1960s and 1970s as an example. During this period, the U.S. faced a host of challenges, including major military operations in Southeast Asia, wars in the Middle East and South Asia, oil crises in 1973-74 and in 1979, rising inflation, rising unemployment, and multiple recessions. The S&P 500 began 1966 at 93.14 points, and, following many ups and downs, it closed on August 2, 1982, at 103.71—representing a rise of just 11% *over 16 years,* not including dividends. In fact, even after including dividends over those years, the stock market return was actually *-0.4* after adjusting for the high rate of inflation. Anyone who put money into the stock market in 1966 actually lost money by the end of 1981, after taking into consideration rising prices.[17]

In contrast, from 1982 through 1999, the S&P 500 enjoyed spectacular returns, growing from 103 in 1982 to reach a high of 1,527.46 on March 24, 2000, or 15 times its August 1982 value. Including dividends, between 1982 and the peak in March 2000, the S&P 500 returned an astounding 17.3% annually. Had you invested $10,000 in 1982, this would have turned into over $250,000 by the end of 1999. Indeed, between 1995 and 1999, the S&P 500 returned *over 20% each year.*

But even during this long-term "bull" market (when the general trend of the market was up), there were several sudden and dramatic declines, including a drop of over *22% in one day* on October 19, 1987. After each decline, the markets recovered and often quickly went higher, adding to the excitement of the era. In the 1990s, many factors helped propel the markets upward: falling inflation and commodities prices, the end of the Cold War, and new technologies that offered greater efficiencies for businesses. Investors were excited as we approached the dawn of the 21st Century and all the possibilities it offered. With markets peaking, however, some were becoming concerned that the stock market had increased too quickly despite the seemingly new and peaceful era.

In a speech in December 1996, Federal Reserve Chairman Alan Greenspan rhetorically asked about the potential impact of what he saw as investors' "irrational exuberance" on the broader economy. "Clearly, sustained low inflation implies less uncertainty about the future, and lower risk premiums imply higher prices of stocks and other earning assets...But how do we know when irrational exuberance has unduly escalated asset values, which then become subject to unexpected and prolonged contractions as they have in Japan over the past decade?"[18]

Chairman Greenspan was referring to the Japanese stock and real-estate markets, which in the 1980s had enjoyed huge gains. The Nikkei 225, a major index of Japanese companies, had *quadrupled* in five years and peaked at 38,915.87 on December 29, 1989. Following several recessions in the 1990s, when Chairman Greenspan gave his speech in late 1996 the Nikkei was hovering around 19,000, half of its value seven years earlier. (And the Nikkei kept falling. In mid-November 2002, the index hit a new low of 8,197, a 79% drop in 14 years. At the end of 2009, on the 20-year anniversary of the popping of the Japanese bubble, the Nikkei closed at 10,546.*)

Always careful with his words, Chairman Greenspan highlighted the reasons for exceptionally strong U.S. stock market performance in the 1990s, while also warning that investors could become overly excited—exhibiting "irrational

---

* Despite the long decline of the Nikkei in Japan, the "Europe, Asia, and Far East" index fund—what the I Fund is based on and which holds significant amount of Japanese stocks—had an annualized return of over 4% in that same 20-year period through 2009, with double-digit returns in the early 2000s. While this is not spectacular, it shows that even as stock markets in one country experience dramatic declines, growth in other areas can more than make up for the losses.

exuberance"—based on assumptions that the stock market would continue to go up in the foreseeable future, just because it had risen dramatically over the past 15 years. In pointing out that the Japanese stock market was experiencing a prolonged decline, Chairman Greenspan was implying that a future decline in U.S. stock markets was not impossible, either.

Perhaps the ultimate warning came in late 1999, when Warren Buffett predicted very low market returns into the early 2000s. Buffett wrote in his 1999 letter to Berkshire Hathaway shareholders that it was a "virtual certainty" that the S&P 500 "will do far less well in the next decade or two than it has done since 1982."[19] Buffett echoed this prediction in a November 22, 1999 *Fortune Magazine* interview that, after factoring inflation, stocks might return 4% over the next decade.[20]

Thus, in late 1999, Warren Buffett warned on multiple occasions that, instead of average returns in the double-digits (12%, 15%, even 18% as some were predicting into the foreseeable future), the *best* investors could hope for was an annual return of 4% into the 2010s, after inflation. Moreover, returns could be less than 4%, as he emphasized in the *Fortune* article.

Ten years after these predictions were published, it turned out that Buffett was correct in his forecast. With the bursting of the Internet bubble, the attacks of 9/11, subsequent allied military actions, and a relatively mild recession in the United States in 2001-2002, the S&P 500 suffered three years of significant declines in a row. The S&P 500 inched slowly upward from early 2003, but after barely making new highs in late 2007 the market then fell back again in 2008 and early 2009, and at the end of 2010 it still hadn't fully recovered from the losses in the early 2000s. (Following steep market declines in late 2008, however, Buffett declared in a *New York Times* op-ed that he was now buying stocks of American companies, issuing a new and more bullish forecast for the 2010s and 2020s.[21])

Thus, the current period of stagnation and periodic downturns—like the extended stagflation during 1966-1982—is a time when the stock markets return to their historical averages following years of "irrational exuberance." This is called "reversion to the mean"—that is, long periods of extraordinary growth that are followed by long periods of stagnation, as the markets revert to their long-term average growth rate. The longer the periods of exceptional growth, the longer the periods of potential market stagnation.

And, paradoxically, periods of sudden decline or long stagnation can be the best times to invest in the markets, because prices become increasingly cheaper over time. Just as we all like to buy things when they are "on sale," all things being equal, so it is with investing in the stock and bond markets. It is more advantageous in the long run to invest money when investments are cheaper, rather than when they are more expensive. We will explore ways to buy into declining markets later in this book.

TSP RISKS YOU *DON'T* HAVE

It is important to know that, by investing in the indexed TSP funds, one risk you *don't* face is company-specific risk, that is, the risk that you will lose *all* your money by investing it in one company's stock. Investing in one stock is very risky because if the company goes bust, so does your investment! Even big companies can fail, and quite dramatically too: Enron, MCI, and Adelphia were some of the major companies that went bankrupt in the aftermath of the Internet bubble in the early 2000s, while Lehman Brothers and a host of regional banks went bankrupt during the financial crisis in 2008 and 2009. Thousands of investors lost all of their money invested in these companies.

The TSP stock funds, however, invest in hundreds of companies, and it is impossible for them all to go bankrupt at the same time. Some companies might do poorly for some time, and the market might decline for fairly long periods as a result, but you will never risk losing *all* of your money by investing in and holding TSP stock funds. And over time, the TSP stock funds can recover and continue their upward trends. We will discuss this a little further in the next chapter.

Also, because these are *index* funds with transparent trading policies and because one individual does *not* control them, there is no chance of losing money in a Bernard Madoff-type ponzi scheme. Recall that investment funds controlled by Madoff had for decades provided relatively high returns, before Madoff admitted in December 2008 that his investment funds were really a scam and that he was taking money from new investors to pay returns to longer-term investors—and skimming millions for his own use! This type of fraud in any of the TSP funds would be impossible because of the stringent auditing and transparency of the investments.

The Greatest Risk – Not Saving! For all these risks noted above, the greatest risk is to *not save* and to not invest *anything at all*. If you don't save and invest during your career, you will have literally nothing in your older years, aside from a very basic government pension—nothing for yourself, and no financial legacy to pass on to your children or to your favorite charities.

Tragically, the personal savings rate in the United States dropped to near-zero in the early 2000s. In 2005, the savings rate dropped briefly to -0.7%—meaning that a majority of people borrowed and spent more than they made in personal income. This is the first time since the early years of the Great Depression—1932 and 1933—that the savings rate in the U.S. actually dropped into *negative* territory. While the savings rate recovered to approximately 6% by 2010, it is too soon to tell whether this trend will continue.

The U.S. savings rate has fallen steadily to zero since 1980—and in the third quarter of 2005, the savings rate fell to -0.7%, the first negative savings rate since 1933! (source: U.S. Bureau of Economic Analysis).

Because of low savings rates, the average household wealth has remained relatively stagnant since at least the mid-1990s. This is certainly the case for those under 35, while those between the ages of 35 to 44 have experienced little growth in their household wealth, as well. Only those 55 and over have enjoyed some growth in their household wealth:

	1995	**1998**	**2001**	**2004**
Under 35	$14,800	$10,600	$12,500	$14,200
35-44	$64,200	$73,500	$82,600	$69,400
45-54	$116,800	$122,300	$141,600	$144,700
55-64	$141,900	$148,200	$197,400	$248,700
65-74	$136,600	$169,800	$189,400	$190,100
Over 75	$114,500	$145,600	$165,400	$163,100

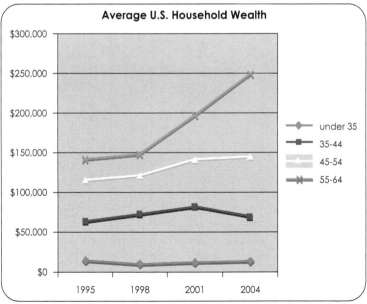

Median U.S. household wealth has remained stagnant since the early 1990s, especially for those under 45 years of age (source: Board of Governors Federal Reserve System, "2004 Survey of Consumer Finances," February 28, 2006).

This is unfortunate because, despite all ↘
downs of the stock markets over the past 50 ye
amount invested each year would have yielded a   ~g
results over long periods of time. As illustrated i ↙ a later
chapter and in the appendix to this book, a person investing just $1,000 at the beginning of 1970 in the S&P 500,
and who increased that same contribution by 5% in January
each year over the following 40 years (from age 25 to 65, for
example) would have almost $1 million at the end of 2010,
despite the stagnant stock markets in the 1970s and 2000s.

In terms of saving and investing, Federal Government
employees are doing a good job at contributing money
to their TSP accounts. According to an analysis of TSP
accounts by the Federal Retirement Thrift Investment Board
(FRTIB)—the body that oversees the Thrift Savings Plan—
participation rates have steadily increased over the years.
In 2005, 88.8% of all FERS employees contributed money
to their TSP accounts, with participation by those under 30
growing from 76.3% in 2000 to 83.8% in 2005. This com-
pares with 91.7% of those 60 to 69 who contribute. The
average contribution rate was a healthy 8.6% of base salary
in 2005, ranging from an average 6.4% contribution rate
among those under 30 to over 11% for older participants.
For CSRS employees, who are not eligible for a government match because of their larger pensions, approximately
67% contributed a portion of their income to the TSP.[22]

Average accounts continue to grow, as well. The average
account for all active participants was $37,493 in 2006, and
for those 40 to 44 years of age with 20 or more years of service,
the average account was just over $138,000 by early 2008.[23] By
the end of 2010, 136 TSP accounts had *over $1 million*, with
one TSP account owner having close to $4 million![24] Granted,
some of those TSP account owners had probably transferred some funds from long-established, traditional 401(k)

accounts in the private sector, but this illustrates that, with steady contributions over long periods of time, it is possible for a TSP investor to build wealth in the millions of dollars.

But with close to an 89% participation rate among FERS employees, over one in ten FERS employees were still *not* participating. Those individuals are forgoing the automatic government match to their contributions of up to 5%. They are losing out on *free* money. When asked why they were not contributing, over 14% said they were "saving in other ways," despite eligibility for a government matching contribution in the TSP just for contributing. Another 20% said they did not "have enough money to contribute," though a contribution rate of even 1% or 2% of salary can help build decent personal savings over the long term.[25] As of mid-2010, new Federal Government workers are now automatically enrolled in the TSP with 3% contributions from their biweekly pay automatically going to the G Fund, so participation rates will rise further.

However, the FRTIB found that in 2005, those under 30 years of age had a large portion of their TSP account allocated to the G Fund. This was probably due to newer participants not taking an active role in allocating their investments among the different funds, yet this age group especially has the most to gain from decades of potential growth in the stock funds.

And while a full two-thirds of CSRS participants are contributing to the TSP, the one-third of the remaining CSRS participants are losing out on tax-deferred growth of their potential contributions, assuming they are not participating in any other tax-deferred savings plans. (Even if they are participating in other tax-deferred plans, they will not find any broad-based stock or bond mutual funds that are cheaper than those in the TSP.) Similarly, as of mid-2010 over 550,000 uniformed personnel were contributing a portion of their pay to their TSP accounts, representing just over 37% of the approximately 1.5 million service men and women who are eligible to contribute.[26]

Ultimately, saving and investing, even a little at a time, provides many benefits for you, your family, and for the nation as a whole.

By saving and investing steadily over time, you can grow an increasingly substantial financial cushion for you and your family in your older years. This has a remarkable psychological benefit, because the more you have saved and invested, the more you feel in control of your own financial independence. And the more you have control over your own finances, the more secure you feel in your personal life. By saving and investing, you are also setting a solid foundation for a more secure future for you and your family—you are building a *legacy*.

With the TSP, you can check your account any time. It is completely transparent: you know exactly what you have and how it has grown over the years. And the more you contribute, the more your TSP account grows. This is not the case with a pension benefit, as it is a simple function of calculating one percent or so per year of work multiplied by the average of your highest three years' salaries for civilian employees, or around 50% of your base salary after 20 or more years for uniformed employees depending on when you leave service. No more, no less. With the TSP, you choose how much you save and where you put it, and thus, you have more control over (but also have more risk related to) how you build your wealth over time.

Importantly, you can also take the money with you if you decide to change jobs, and you can continue to grow your investments even as you explore new career opportunities. You are no longer locked in the "golden handcuffs" of lifetime employment with the Federal Government. You can continue to build your savings and investments no matter how many jobs you have over your lifetime. While your pension benefit remains the same between the time you leave government service and the time you begin to collect it, you can continue to add to your TSP money even after you leave government service as long as you roll it over into an Individual Retirement Account (IRA), which is a relatively easy process to accomplish. Or you can keep it in the TSP, and invest separately in an IRA.

Finally, by saving and investing in the TSP, you are buying U.S. Government bonds and the bonds and stocks of U.S. companies. This is very healthy for the U.S. economy, because these entities need our investments to continue to build and improve their products and services. And, if you invest in foreign companies through the I Fund, you are investing in the world economy, as well.

Ultimately, the TSP is an incredibly convenient and extremely cost-effective means for Federal Government employees to build wealth in a fully transparent and portable way.

Pre-Investment Strategies

We have briefly reviewed the advantages of the Thrift Savings Plan as a wealth-building mechanism, as well as the advantages and risks of any investing program. Through the strategies presented in the following chapters, I hope to further arm you, the TSP investor, with the knowledge to recognize various opportunities while, at the same time, lessening the risks involved in investing over the long term.

Before getting started, I'd like to present two "Pre-Investment Strategies." These Pre-Investment Strategies will help early TSP investors build a solid foundation for future growth, as we begin to explore the five main Strategies presented in this book.

Pre-Investment Strategy 1: If possible, contribute at least 5% of your salary to your TSP account.

- For FERS participants, the 5% contribution means you are eligible for the full government match, no matter what your salary may be. For CSRS participants and uniformed personnel, the 5% contribution will be in addition to your richer pension benefits, meaning that you will be able to build even more wealth over your career.
- If you simply cannot contribute 5%—and I understand this situation well, since for the first six months of my government career I was unable to contribute 5%—try to contribute 1% or 2%, just to get in the habit of contributing even a very limited amount. You will start to see some growth both in your salary and in your TSP account, and you can increase your contributions slowly as you become more comfortable financially.

Pre-Investment Strategy 2: Build a basic emergency fund of at least one month's expenses untouched in an FDIC-insured * bank account.

- An emergency fund will help you pay for unexpected expenses without having to cut back on your TSP contributions suddenly. The emergency fund will also provide you with more peace of mind, as you establish yourself financially.

Now that we've taken a look at the TSP, as well as the importance of developing long-term savings and investing strategies to lessen the risks involved, let's now take a look at Strategy I to determine your level of interest in investing and your relative tolerance for risk.

---

* FDIC stands for "Federal Deposit Insurance Corporation," which as of 2010 insures bank accounts up to $250,000 in the unlikely event of a bank failure.

STRATEGY I – ASSESS YOUR LEVEL OF INTEREST AND RISK TOLERANCE

Now that we've reviewed the basics of the Thrift Savings Plan, let's begin with Strategy I for investing in the TSP. Before deciding on which TSP funds to invest in, the TSP investor should assess his or her level of interest in investing and identify tolerance for risk.

Identifying your tolerance for risk is particularly important, since success of the subsequent strategies in this book will be based on how much you can tolerate of the sometimes wide swings in the TSP funds.

Upon determining your interest in actively following your TSP investments and your tolerance for risk, Strategy II will help you to decide how to allocate your investments among the TSP funds. Once you have allocated your TSP investments among the TSP funds, Strategies III and IV will help you to decide how to readjust your TSP investments periodically, since some funds do better than others over time and during different market conditions. Finally, Strategy V will provide a few more investment options to help you build even more wealth during your government service and beyond.

The flow chart below illustrates how answering the questions in Strategy I will help to determine how to use strategies II-IV:

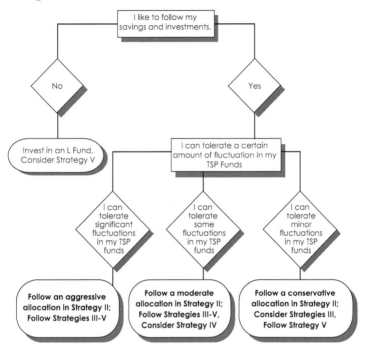

Rate Your Level of Interest in the Stock and Bond Markets

The first step in Strategy I is to determine your interest in investing. This is a fairly simple process. Simply ask yourself whether you like to check your TSP account periodically, and whether you like to check on how the financial markets are doing from time to time.

This doesn't mean you have to be *passionate* about investing, because quite frankly, most of the time the money in your TSP account is not doing much of anything. It is often said that investing can be like watching paint dry, but watching your investments can be even more boring, because at least paint dries in less than a day! With your TSP, you'll add a couple hundred dollars every few weeks or every month, and maybe it goes up or down a percentage or two over a couple of weeks or a couple of months, but that's it. Being comfortable with the often-mundane task of following your TSP funds—and the financial markets—over time is important, however, as varying market conditions will require readjusting of TSP funds at times.

Here are a few questions to help you gauge your interest in investing:

	Yes	No

1) I like to check my TSP account every few weeks.

2) I like to check how the U.S. and international stock and bond markets are doing from time to time.

3) I like to read books on investing strategies to try to improve my investment results.

4) When I hear the word "market," I think of buying fresh fruits and vegetables, not stocks and bonds.

If you answered "Yes" to at least two of the first three questions, skim through the next section describing the L Funds and proceed to the section after that. You are interested in investing.

If, however, you answered "No" to the first three questions and "Yes" to the last one, perhaps one of the TSP's "L Funds" is right for you.

Consider Investing in an L Fund

If you don't like actively following your investments, that's ok! No need to force yourself to do what you don't enjoy doing. You've got other things to do with your time, and you don't want to have to remember to check how this or that fund did over the past couple of days or weeks.

Luckily, the TSP offers a special type of fund for those who prefer to take a more passive approach to investing.

In 2005, the TSP introduced a group of funds called "life cycle funds," which automatically shift investments among the TSP funds over one's career from growth-oriented stock funds to more conservative bond funds.

When you are younger, your TSP money is invested in more growth-oriented stock funds, so that you might enjoy some growth of your investments in your early years of investing in the TSP. As you age, the money is gradually shifted to more stable, higher-yielding bond funds. This way, when you are ready to start withdrawing your money in your 60s or 70s, you will not have to be concerned that sudden and steep losses in the growth-oriented (and riskier) stock funds will impact your now more-conservative and stable L Fund. This is all done automatically, and all you have to do once you've decided to invest in an L Fund is set your biweekly or monthly contribution amount and continue to put money into the fund on a regular basis.

As noted in the previous chapter, there are multiple L Funds with "target" dates that are set at ten-year increments, between 2020 and 2050. There is also an L Fund for those who are ready to withdraw their TSP money now—the L Income Fund. As an example of how the L Funds are designed to operate over long periods of time, let's briefly examine how the L 2040 shifts its investments from the time it was started to its target year of 2040.

When it was first set up in 2005, the L 2040 Fund was most heavily weighted toward the TSP stock funds. It had 85% invested in the three stock funds, with 42% in the C Fund, 25% in the I Fund, and 18% in the S Fund. The remaining 15% was invested in the G and F Funds. The amount allocated to the stock funds shift gradually downward each year thereafter, so that in ten years from its establishment—in 2015—the fund will have 75% of TSP investors' money allocated to the three stock funds and 25% allocated to the bond funds. This gradual shift will continue over the years and, by 2035—five years before the target date of 2040—the fund will have 50% in the stock funds and 50% in the bond funds, with 43% of the entire amount in the very stable G Fund. By 2040, the target date for this L Fund, it will have 80% of its holdings in the bond funds and just 20% in the stock funds (and 74% of the L 2040 Fund will be in the very stable G Fund). The fund still allocates some money to the stock funds after 2040 to provide a percentage point or two of growth each year, even as the L Fund investor withdraws money on a regular basis.

The other L funds follow this same process but shift money from the stock funds to the bond funds earlier; the 2020 L Fund will shift a majority of its investments to the bond funds by 2020, while the 2030 L Fund will shift a majority of its investments to the bond funds by 2030.

Since the shift is pre-determined, the L Fund investor does not need to worry about how much to put in each of the TSP stock and bond funds. These decisions are already made for you, and they are done in such a way that you will most likely enjoy decent growth in your investments over time when you are young, while later your investments become more conservative as you are closer to an age when you might want to withdraw money from your TSP account in your post-career years. You just invest all of your biweekly or monthly contributions in one of the L Funds, and you are done.

Once that decision is made, you can just watch your money grow over the years of your government service and beyond.

After deciding to invest in one of the L Funds, the next step is to decide which L Fund to choose. Since the funds gradually shift from growth to income over several decades, L Fund investors generally try to match the year of the L Fund with their expected withdrawal date, sometime after they turn 59½ years old when they can take it out as they choose. If the L Fund investor planned to begin to withdraw some of the money after turning 60 in 2038, the L 2040 fund might be the best fund in which to invest. If the investor turns 60 in 2033, perhaps the L 2030 fund is right, although the L 2040 might be better suited for those who expect to stay in the work force into their 60s and 70s.

Indeed, much of your decision will depend on how long you plan to continue working. If you think you will likely continue to work in the years after you turn 60 and will leave your TSP account untouched, you should probably consider rounding up to the higher L Fund target year. If you think you'll want to begin to withdraw the money sooner after turning 60, you might want to consider rounding down.

This is not an exact science, as none of us can know when we will actually need to begin to withdraw money from the TSP. Our personal health, our family, our professional situation, and other factors in our late 50s and 60s will all play a role in our decision process at that point. If you are simply unsure about when you might want to begin withdrawing from your TSP account, and you are a cautious person by nature, perhaps it is better to choose an L Fund that is rounded down from the year when you turn 60.

Also, it is important to note that there will still be some volatility in your L Fund account, especially for those who invest in the L 2040 and L 2050 Funds. These funds allocate more to the stock funds within the TSP that tend to rise and fall in value more than the bond funds, and so your L Fund will also rise and fall more as a result. This is to be expected, but ov the years the value of your L Fund will increase, despite the day-to-day gyrations of the markets, as you continue to add money to your TSP account through biweekly contributions.

The chart below shows the percentage gains or losses in each of the L Funds from 2005 to 2010. Notice that in 2008, all the L funds experienced some losses, with the L 2040 losing almost one-third of its value before recovering the following two years.

	L Income	L 2020	L 2030	L 2040
2005	2.15	3.4	3.59	3.92
2006	7.59	13.72	15	16.53
2007	5.56	6.87	7.14	7.36
2008	-5.09	-22.77	-27.5	-31.53
2009	8.57	19.14	22.48	25.19
2010	5.74	10.59	12.48	13.89

If you have decided to invest in one of the Lifecycle Funds, you can read further in this chapter to gain a better understanding of volatility—the ups and downs—of the TSP stock funds especially. Or, if you feel like you have enough of an understanding about the L Funds and wish to move forward with your investing strategies, you can skip the chapters for Strategies II-IV and continue to Strategy V for additional investing ideas.

For the More Active Investor: Rate Your Risk Tolerance

For those who want to take a more active role in choosing how to invest money among the various TSP funds, the next step is to determine how much risk you are willing to take.

Some TSP funds are "riskier" than others, as they rise or decline in value more than other funds. Risk, here, is

...w much and how rapidly a given TSP fund ...creases in value over a given timeframe. The ..., S, and I) are in general riskier than the bond funds (G and F), because the stock funds can go up or down quite dramatically, by several percentage points or more on any given day and by 10%, 20%, or more in any given year. The bond funds, in contrast, do not gain or lose value as dramatically. But if history is any indication, over very long periods of time—several decades—the stock funds do provide a greater return than the bond funds.

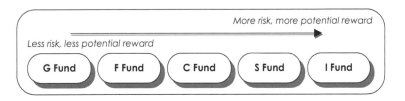

The G Fund is the least risky of the group, because it invests in safer—but low-return—U.S. Government bonds. The fund's return has been limited to the mid-single digits (just over 4% on average 2001-2010), but its value is stable and fairly predictable over time. The F Fund, also a bond fund, is slightly more risky (slightly more volatile) than the G Fund, because it invests in U.S. corporate and mortgage bonds, in addition to U.S. Government-backed bonds. While its return has usually been a percentage or two higher than the G Fund, it can fluctuate more in value (even decrease in value at times) and, thus, is less predictable than the G Fund.

Among the stock funds, the S and I funds are more risky than the C Fund, because they can be more volatile due to the smaller size of the companies (the S Fund) and the need to invest in other currencies besides the dollar (the I

Fund). The stocks of smaller corporations can rise and fall more than larger ones because it is easier for institutional investors to buy and sell relatively larger chunks of a smaller company's stock, thus driving the price of the stock up or down more. And in order to invest in international corporations in the I Fund, the I Fund must buy stocks according to their prices in euros, pound sterling, yen, and other currencies, and these currencies gain and lose value relative to the dollar separately from the price of company stocks. If a company's stock price falls as the country's local currency weakens, the investment in dollars will decrease even more dramatically than if the stock price had fallen in dollars.

Over the very long term, those who take more risk in an intelligent and disciplined manner are rewarded more for their efforts. In fact, Thomas Stanley and William Danko, authors of *The Millionaire Next Door*, found that a large majority of the millionaires they surveyed—95%—invested in stock.[27] Stock markets have historically returned more than bond markets. Thus, to truly build wealth it is important to embrace some risk by investing in at least one of the TSP's stock funds. By accepting a certain level of risk, a person can be rewarded with greater returns over a 30- or 40-year work and investing career. There are ways to reduce risk while earning a higher rate of return by investing in multiple TSP funds, which we will examine in greater detail in Strategy II.

At the same time, one should not take on *too much* risk in anticipation of significant returns in the stock funds, as a severe market decline might cause the unprepared or novice investor to sell most or all of his or her stock funds prematurely, to avoid what they fear will be further losses. This is exactly what the long-term investor *should not do*— sell when the stock funds are declining—as this will compound losses and severely hinder the building of wealth.

The Peril of Unrealistic Expectations

In 2007, the TSP reported that the C Fund had returned around 11.3% annually over the previous 20 years, while the G Fund had returned 6.5% over this same timeframe. To illustrate the difference in returns that this generates, $100,000 invested in the C Fund in 1988 would have grown to almost $851,000 20 years later, while that same amount invested in the G Fund would be worth just over $352,000 20 years later. This is a difference of almost $500,000. All things being equal, you, the rational investor, would of course prefer to have been invested in the higher-returning C Fund over the low-returning G Fund.

Because the C Fund seemingly provided exceptional returns for those who invested in it 20 years ago, it would be easy to "project" or assume that the C Fund will have the same return each and every year in future years as well. Based on this, the novice investor might put all of his money in the C Fund, thinking that, in the next five, ten, or 20 years, he will have enjoyed a return of over 11%.

This is a mistake, however, as this projection was based on an unrealistic expectation that these returns would continue in the future. This annualized rate of return does not mean that the C Fund has returned 11.3% each and every year throughout its history—far from it. The 11.3% annual return of the C Fund over the previous 20 years is just the average annualized return over one 20-year period. This includes returns of over 37%, 22%, and 33% respectively in 1995-1997, and losses of over 9%, 11%, and 22% respectively in 2000-2002.

When one looks at the history of U.S. stock market returns for each five, ten, and 20-year period over the past 100 years, it becomes clear that some periods have had greater returns, while others have had much worse returns. The U.S. stock market has even experienced several bad 20-year timeframes.

Best and Worst Average Yearly Returns of...

Large-Cap Stocks (similar to the C Fund)

	Best return...	Worst return...
5-year return	+28.55% (1995-1999)	-12.47% (1928-1932)
10-year return	+20.06% (1949-1958)	-0.89% (1929-1938)
20-year return	+17.87% (1980-1999)	+3.11% (1929-1948)

Source: Ibbotson Associates, "Stocks, Bonds, Bills, and Inflation 2006 Yearbook,"
p 41.

The worst 20-year period started in 1929. Had you invested $100,000 then, your total return 20 years later would have been just over $186,196 by 1948—very clearly *less* than the 11%-plus returns that grew to $851,000 in the 20 years after the TSP created the C Fund in 1988. And as you can see in the chart above, there have been some five- and even ten-year periods when the S&P 500 actually *declined* in total value.

Bond funds can also go up and down in value over time, but less so than stock funds. The best 20-year period for intermediate-term bonds similar to those held in the G and F funds, for example, is 9.97% each year on average from 1981-2000. The worst return was from 1940-1959, when bonds returned just 1.58% on average each of those years.

Intermediate-Term Govt. Bonds

	Best return...	Worst return...
5-year return	+16.98% (1982-1986)	+0.96% (1955-1959
10-year return	+13.13% (1982-1991)	+1.25% (1947-1956)
20-year return	+9.97% (1981-2000)	+1.58% (1940-1959)

Source: Ibbotson Associates, "Stocks, Bonds, Bills, and Inflation 2006 Yearbook,"
p 41.

Thus, over some long-term periods, any or all of the TSP funds might do very well, creating the unrealistic expectation that those same funds will continue to do similarly well in the foreseeable future. If an investor is unprepared for dramatic and/or long periods of bad market returns in her chosen TSP funds over several years—up to 20 years or longer—she might give up investing in the TSP stock funds and put everything into the G Fund, which enjoys consistent—but low—monthly returns with no possibility for growth. By doing so, this investor would miss eventual and potentially sizable gains, as the stock funds recover from a long period of low returns.

The converse is also true. During some long periods of time, some of the TSP funds might do very poorly, again creating the unrealistic expectation that the funds will continue to do very poorly into the distant future. During this time, the novice investor might continue to invest heavily in the "safer" funds—i.e., the funds that have performed relatively better in the past few years—while avoiding the poorly performing funds.

Both of these investment plans are mistaken for several reasons. First, by shifting all of our money into the G Fund after suffering unexpected declines in the other funds, we would realize a loss from the declining funds (see next box). Second, we would miss out on sudden growth spurts that come when we least expect them—and these sudden recoveries take even the so-called experts appearing in the popular media by surprise. Stock funds sometimes decline quite significantly, but they can recover and go even higher very quickly, as well. Just as we do not know when any of the TSP funds will go down or for how long, it is impossible to know when any of the funds will go back up, and oftentimes, funds go up very quickly when people least expect it. The successful TSP investor will avoid realizing losses by not selling a fund when it is down significantly.

When The TSP Funds Decline, Have You Really "Lost" Anything?

It is important to remain aware that a *decline* in any given TSP fund is not the same thing as a *loss*. A *decline* in a fund becomes a *loss* when you transfer money out of the TSP fund into another fund. If you do not transfer any money out of the declining fund, but rather hold on to it until it recovers, you will not lose anything!

Instead of thinking of your TSP account as similar to a regular bank account, where a smaller amount of money means that you have less money to withdraw, think of your TSP investments like the house in which you live. Your house is a real asset: it has a value, and you can sell it when you want. The value of your house changes over time; sometimes the value falls, but it usually rises, over long periods of time. If you do not need or want to sell it, the value of your house is irrelevant to your day-to-day finances. You just keep paying the mortgage and sleep soundly, knowing that it is yours. You can, of course, refinance your mortgage to take money out for, say, a kitchen renovation or to build an addition to your home, but refinancing is, in effect, selling the rights to some of the value of your house to the bank in return for cash for other projects.

Thus, would you sell your house just because the housing market began to decline, or because the housing market had declined for several years in a row? Most likely, no. If you did not need to move, you would most likely keep your house until the market recovered, when your house could sell for a better price—and you could make more money on the sale.

Yet some people make this mistake when stock markets decline. They sell some or all of their funds after a decline in the mistaken idea that this action will protect the remaining portion of their money. But it is the *act of selling* that causes the losses. And then, once the market has "recovered," that is, once prices have moved back up to their original value, some will put money back into the funds that had already recovered. This would be the same as selling your house when the housing market had collapsed and then buying a new house after the price of houses have gone back up again. This action is not rational.

By not panicking and sticking to your investment strategies until the markets recover—and markets have in the past always recovered, given time—then you will be able to weather down markets and even perhaps increase your investments with periodic additions in the process.

The best defense against the risk of a falling fund is to diversify your TSP holdings strategically among the different TSP funds, discussed further in Strategy II. This should be done based on one's ability to weather declines in one's total TSP account.

But before moving on to allocation strategies, we should first determine what kind of investor you are by gauging your reaction to a significantly declining market, based on two scenarios detailed below.

How Much Risk Should You Take? Gauging Your Reaction to a Severely Declining Market

To remain successful in any long-term savings and investment program, you should be able to stick to your chosen investment and savings strategy through good times and bad. Sticking to a growth-oriented investment strategy can be especially difficult during sharp market declines, because you will watch your TSP account drop 10%, 20%, or more in a fairly short period of time. And, as the months and perhaps years pass, it might seem like the market—and your TSP investments—will never go back up in value. But those who decide to change their TSP investment allocation during a severe market decline will suffer potentially serious losses in their TSP accounts.

In one dramatic example, what if you considered yourself very comfortable with market risk and invested 100% of your TSP savings in the C Fund in 1987? While the S&P 500 rose dramatically during the first half of the year, following a few months of significant declines you would have awakened one day to discover the value of your account had dropped by almost *one-fourth in one day!* With $100,000 invested in the C Fund, a drop of this magnitude would mean that your account would now be worth around $77,000. Overnight. This happened on October 19, 1987, when the stock market fell almost 23% in one trading session. And this sudden decline was not limited to U.S. stock markets; international stock markets dropped by similar amounts. Investments in the C, F, and I funds all would have been affected.

Is this the kind of market risk that you are prepared to encounter? And what if the markets keep falling, even after such a spectacular one-day plunge? Would you sell all of your stock holdings in the hopes of keeping the remaining amount safe, or would you view the drop as an opportunity to add more to your investments for even greater potential future returns?

After the October 1987 crash, the S&P 500 fully recovered within a year and continued to increase thereafter. Had an investor put money into stock funds immediately after world stock markets plunged that day in October, he or she would have enjoyed a significant double-digit return on that investment in a very short period of time. But to do so, an investor would have to maintain faith in his or her investment strategy to survive the immediate aftermath of this type of market plunge.

As you undertake a long-term investment program such as the TSP, it is critical that you understand how you would react during periods of steep declines in your investment account. It is easy to remain invested in the stock funds when they might increase by 10% or 15% a year or more, but how will you react when they are *falling* by 10% or 15% or more? While some investors embrace risk and are comfortable with investing a majority of their savings in stock funds—and they believe they can weather significant drops in their investment accounts—others might prefer a more balanced investment strategy to smooth out the ups and downs of the stock and bond markets. However, it is difficult to know in advance how you might react to a significant downturn in the markets if you have not yet experienced one.

To determine your level of risk tolerance, let's take a look at how you might react in two scenarios during a period of significant market fluctuation.

In the first scenario below, you will experience a significant market decline while fully invested in the C Fund. In the more conservative second scenario, you will experience the same market decline with half of your portfolio in the C Fund and the other half in the G Fund. I won't reveal yet when this timeframe took place, but it is important to keep in mind that these market swings *really happened.* (And no, this is not a recounting of the 2008-2009 market decline.) As you read the scenarios, think to yourself how you might have reacted as your hypothetical TSP account balance fluctuated during this time.

Scenario 1: the C Fund*

At the beginning of the year, you have $100,000 invested in the C Fund. You've worked hard for a number of years to save and invest this money and have enjoyed watching your TSP account grow over the years. Indeed, the C Fund has enjoyed significant growth over the past number of years, although over the last couple of years there have been a few steep drops. But each time the market has recovered, and the previous year saw a 20% gain before dropping slightly at the end of the year.

Despite the recent ups and downs of the market, you have decided to stay invested in this fund because of its long-term average growth of over 10% per year—you know at that rate your account will double every seven years or so, even without adding anything to it. It will grow even faster, since you continue to add $250 to it each pay period. You have several decades before you will retire, and at this rate, you expect to retire with over one million dollars in your TSP account, and perhaps even more.

But how well prepared are you mentally for a "bear" market, when the trend of the market is significantly down?

The stock market begins the new year with a sudden downturn, dropping 6% or so through February. This is not so bad—you understand that the stock funds can sometimes go down 10% or more every few years, so drops like this are to be expected. Besides, you are contributing $250 each pay period so you are buying into the declining market as shares are progressively cheaper. Given the drop in the market, though, your TSP account has gradually declined some through the end of March:

---

* Returns for the C Fund over this period were calculated using the Friday closing price for the S&P 500, with the $250 biweekly contribution added to the recalculated TSP account total at the end of each pay period. This period does not include the re-investment of dividends.

Pay Period 1, January	**$101,308.87**
Pay Period 2, January	**$99,138.67**
Pay Period 3, February	**$97,881.80**
Pay Period 4, February	**$96,834.44**
Pay Period 5, March	**$97,623.55**
Pay Period 6, March	**$93,661.13**

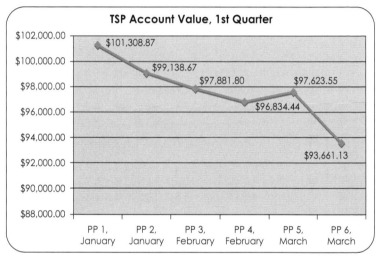

At the beginning of April, your TSP account recovers somewhat to around $97,000. Suddenly, however, at the beginning of May, the market plunges close to 5% in a matter of days, adding to the losses in March. Your account has been cushioned somewhat from greater declines because you've already added $2,250 since the beginning of the year, but as summer vacation approaches, you see that your TSP account is now only worth around $91,000. Even with the money you've added, your $100,000 account has dropped close to 10% in six months. You continue to add $250 each pay period, so the actual loss would have been greater had you not been adding money each pay period. Here is how your account would look through the end of June:

Pay Period 7, April	**$94,255.22**
Pay Period 8, April	**$96,997.88**
Pay Period 9, April	**$96,236.13**
Pay Period 10, May	**$90,295.81**
Pay Period 11, May	**$90,606.67**
Pay Period 12, June	**$91,876.68**
Pay Period 13, June	**$91,392.36**

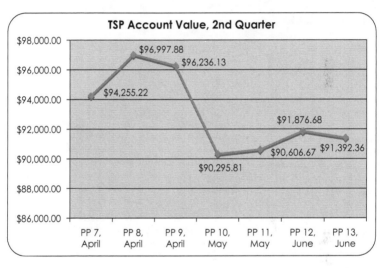

You experience a brief feeling of relief in late July, as the market recovers by 6% and your account is back up to over $96,000. You take a summer vacation in early August, thinking that a recovery is in store. But checking your account after you return, you find that the market has dropped even further and your account is down to $90,046 in a month. The market recovers again somewhat in September, climbing to over $95,000. Here is how your account has fared over the summer months through September:

Pay Period 14, July	**$91,493.34**
Pay Period 15, July	**$96,577.75**
Pay Period 16, August	**$92,580.06**
Pay Period 17, August	**$90,046.56**
Pay Period 18, September	**$93,078.95**
Pay Period 19, September	**$95,496.88**

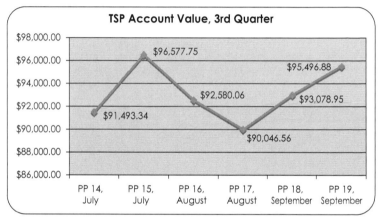

In mid-October you notice quite a gain in your account, as it has increased to $98,000. While this is not a full recovery back to your original $100,000 amount—and you've added an additional $5,250 in total since January—it is a decent gain from six weeks ago.

Unfortunately, the gains do not stick, and the stock market plunges again. By December, the stock market is down for the year over 20%. Your C Fund falls to just over $84,000 before recovering somewhat to end the year at $88,562. You've added $6,500 in biweekly contributions from your paycheck over the year, but your TSP account is still down significantly. Here is how your account performed through the last pay period:

Pay Period 20, October	**$98,107.58**
Pay Period 21, October	**$98,688.02**
Pay Period 22, October	**$96,117.60**
Pay Period 23, November	**$93,503.91**
Pay Period 24, November	**$86,625.00**
Pay Period 25, December	**$84,464.74**
Pay Period 26, December	**$88,562.69**

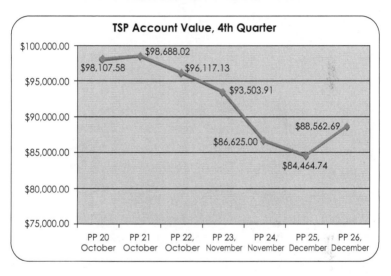

How do you feel?

At this point, ask yourself how you felt as your account continued to fall through the year. Your $100,000 is worth just over $88,000, even after adding $6,500 over the past year. What would your gut be telling you at this point, or at any point during the year?

1) Transfer the entire $88,000 now to the U.S. Government bond fund (the G Fund) to protect what money

you have left from further declines; adjust your biweekly contributions to have everything go to the G Fund.

2) Transfer some of the C Fund now to the G or F bond fund to protect it; adjust your biweekly contributions to put half of the $250 in the bond fund every two weeks, as well.

3) Hold on to the $88,000 in the C Fund and hope that the market will go back up again soon; continue to add $250 to the C Fund each pay period, investing into the declining market for greater gains in the future.

4) Following the adage to "buy low and sell high," look for ways to increase biweekly contributions to invest even more in the C Fund as it continues to drop to improve long-term investment results when the stock market finally recovers (even if it takes years).

There is no "right" answer to the above questions. It is important that you answer these questions honestly, because this type of market might recur in the future. Again, this exercise is to determine how you would react to a severe market decline ahead of time, so as not to panic during a real downturn in the market when your hard-earned TSP savings is really at stake.

Keep these questions in mind as we continue the exercise into the second year, because *the declining market is just getting started.*

The next year begins with even more fluctuations in the stock market. You suffer more declines in your TSP in January, and in February, your account drops below $85,000 for the first time in several years. However, you continue to add $250 faithfully to your account each payday. By March, your account recovers a little and is back to over $90,000. But there is little sign that this market will recover completely in the near future. Here is how your account looks through the end of March:

Pay Period 1, January	$88,289.79
Pay Period 2, January	$88,244.37
Pay Period 3, February	$84,567.53
Pay Period 4, February	$87,620.26
Pay Period 5, March	$90,065.59
Pay Period 6, March	$89,845.83

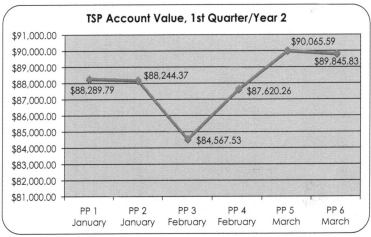

In April, the downturn begins anew, and your TSP account falls a stunning 10% to $81,000. Approaching summer, your account has fallen almost 20% below your original $100,000 account balance of 18 months ago, even after adding $9,750 in new contributions since then. Here is how your TSP account performed through spring and into summer:

Pay Period 7, April	$86,160.98
Pay Period 8, April	$87,096.48
Pay Period 9, April	$85,061.07

Pay Period 10, May	**$82,441.23**
Pay Period 11, May	**$81,822.05**
Pay Period 12, June	**$85,840.66**
Pay Period 13, June	**$81,107.58**

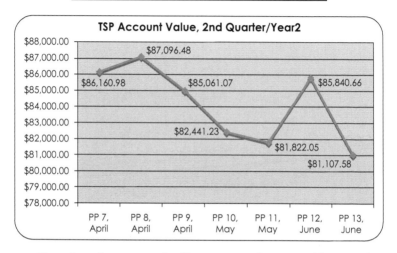

Despite the steep declines over the past 18 months, the downturn *still* does not stop. In late July and early August, your account hovers around $78,000. But then the markets plunge yet again as investors succumb to something close to panic. In late August and into September, your C Fund takes a real beating. At the end of September, your TSP account is now worth just over $60,000. Your account has fallen about 40% by this point, *even after* adding over $11,500 of new money over the past 18 months.

Here is how your account looks through September:

Pay Period 14, July	**$78,669.71**
Pay Period 15, July	**$78,210.12**
Pay Period 16, August	**$76,998.43**

Pay Period 17, August	**$68,383.04**
Pay Period 18, September	**$68,508.79**
Pay Period 19, September	**$67,530.97**
Pay Period 20, September	**$60,271.11**

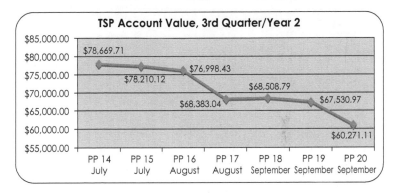

What are you feeling now? Do you wish you had shifted everything from the C Fund to the G Fund at the beginning of the year, or even during the past summer? Your TSP account was worth over $88,000 at the end of last year and averaged nearly $95,000 last summer.

Or, on the other hand, are you wishing you had more money to invest in this severely declining market, feeling that the best time to invest new money is when the market is down significantly?

It is now October. The stock market does not stay down for long. Within days, your TSP account recovers to just over $70,000, although it begins to decline in value again in late November and early December. At the end of December, your account is now worth $69,872. While this is a small recovery from late September, this is still down almost 34% from your original $100,000 account balance two years ago—and after you have added *$13,000 of new money*, $250 every pay period—since then.

Here is how your account looks through the end of year 2:

Pay Period 21, October	**$70,131.23**
Pay Period 22, October	**$71,933.66**
Pay Period 23, November	**$70,265.56**
Pay Period 24, November	**$68,619.93**
Pay Period 25, December	**$66,025.88**
Pay Period 26, December	**$66,344.79**
End of Year, Dec 31:	**$69,872.51**

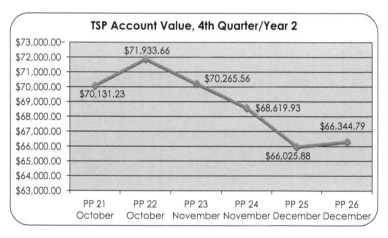

Will the stock market ever recover? Will your TSP account go back up in the next few months, or in a year or two, or will the declines continue? No one can answer this, because no one knows. The experts say the markets always recover eventually, but what does that mean, really? Your $100,000—plus $13,000 in new contributions—is currently worth about $66,000.

Now, how do you **really** *feel?*

Review the questions above again. How do you *really* feel about your account at the end of year two, after your TSP declined by 34% even after adding $13,000 in new money? Would you now, or at any time during the previous year, have done any of the following things?

1) Transfer everything now and put it in the G Fund to protect what money you have left; adjust your biweekly contributions to have everything go to the G Fund.

2) Transfer part of the C Fund into the G or F bond fund to protect that money; adjust your biweekly contributions to put half of the $250 in the bond fund, as well.

3) Keep everything in the C Fund, with the knowledge that the market will recover and go higher at some point in the future; continue to add $250 to the C Fund each pay period.

4) Again, following the adage to "buy low and sell high," look for ways to increase biweekly contributions to invest even more in the C Fund as it continues to drop, to improve investment results over the very long-term when the stock market finally recovers (even if it takes years).

This scenario is taken from the bear market of 1973-1974, when the S&P 500 fell over 14% in 1973 and over 26% in 1974—and when the S&P 500 experienced even steeper declines in August and September 1974 before recovering somewhat at the end of the year. Again, this scenario is important because *it really happened.* Had you invested all your TSP money in the C Fund during years of similar declines, this is how your account would have behaved.

Here is how the S&P 500 looked from 1972 to 1974. Notice that in 1972, the year prior to the two-year example above, the market increased by almost 20% and many people were feeling pretty good about their returns in the stock market. By late 1974, however, some two years later, the market had fallen to half this level before recovering slightly.

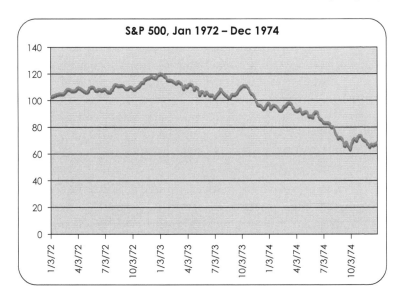

While this type of extended decline happens rarely—once every few decades on average—it does happen from time to time. TSP investors experienced a similarly long, steep market decline in the 2000-2002 period, for example, and another sharp decline in 2008 and in early 2009. The chances are great that we will all experience another similarly steep decline again at least once in our investing lifetimes.

We'll take a look at how this all-stock TSP account would have performed in the 20 years after the 1973-1974 bear market, but let's first see how a TSP account would fare with only half of your money in stocks and the other half in bonds—$50,000 in the C Fund and $50,000 in the G Fund—under these same conditions.

Scenario 2: The C Fund and the G Fund*

The year starts out with some declines in the C Fund in the first few weeks and months of the new year, but you notice the G Fund offers some protection from the declines, since it has remained relatively stable during this time. Ultimately, you see a decline of a few thousand dollars in your total account balance through March, as your TSP account has dropped to $97,405 during these three months. Here is how your account looks during the first few months of the year:

	G Fund	**C Fund**	**Account Total**
Pay period 1, January	$50,110.00	$50,654.44	**$100,764.44**
Pay period 2, January	$50,219.97	$49,569.34	**$99,789.30**
Pay period 3, February	$50,156.64	$48,940.90	**$99,097.54**
Pay period 4, February	$50,093.55	$48,417.22	**$98,510.77**
Pay period 5, March	$50,333.77	$48,811.78	**$99,145.54**
Pay period 6, March	$50,574.54	$46,830.57	**$97,405.10**

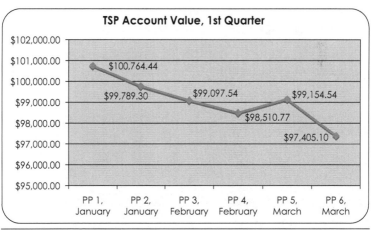

* Since the G Fund did not exist in the early 1970s, the approximate returns of intermediate-term U.S. government bonds in Ibbotson Associates' *Stocks, Bonds, Bills, and Inflation 2006 Yearbook* (p. 245) were used as a substitute.

While your C Fund experiences some further declines into May, falling about 10% in spring to around $45,000, your G Fund has increased somewhat, to $52,000. Through late spring and into summer, your total account remains stagnant as it continues to hover between $97,000 and $99,500. By the end of June, however, despite a 10% decline in the C Fund, your total TSP account is just under $98,000.

Here is how your account looks through June:

	G Fund	C Fund	Account Total
Pay period 7, April	$50,807.43	$47,127.61	**$97,935.04**
Pay period 8, April	$51,040.82	$48,498.94	**$99,539.76**
Pay period 9, April	$51,274.71	$48,118.07	**$99,392.77**
Pay period 10, May	$51,545.84	$45,147.91	**$96,693.74**
Pay period 11, May	$51,817.74	$45,303.34	**$97,121.08**
Pay period 12, June	$51,927.20	$45,938.34	**$97,865.54**
Pay period 13, June	$52,036.62	$45,696.18	**$97,732.80**

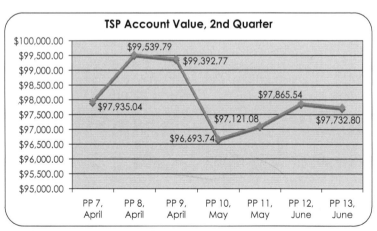

TSP Account Value, 2nd Quarter

As you make final plans for your summer vacation, your TSP account value continues to fluctuate only a few thousand dollars, between $97,000 and $99,000. Soon after your return from vacation, however, you notice that, at the end of September, your account value has actually increased suddenly to over $101,000. Here is how your TSP account fared:

	G Fund	C Fund	Account Total
Pay period 14, July	$51,443.52	$45,746.67	**$97,190.19**
Pay period 15, July	$50,858.60	$48,288.88	**$99,147.47**
Pay period 16, August	$51,629.50	$46,290.03	**$97,919.53**
Pay period 17, August	$52,410.19	$45,023.28	**$97,433.47**
Pay period 18, September	$53,190.32	$46,539.48	**$99,729.80**
Pay period 19, September	$53,980.20	$47,748.44	**$101,728.64**

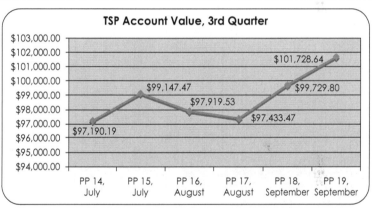

Your total TSP account value continues to increase through mid-October to well over $103,000, driven by a recovery in the C Fund. The balance begins to drop again, however, as Thanksgiving approaches, due especially to another sudden drop in your C Fund. Your G Fund, however, continues to exhibit steady gains. Through the final pay periods of the year, your account balance falls below $100,000 again. At the end of the year the balance levels off to $99,979, almost exactly the same as where your TSP account balance started the year. While your C Fund has declined by around 12%, your G Fund is up by over 10%, with the $6,500 you've added through the year making up the difference:

	G Fund	C Fund	Account Total
Pay period 20, October	$54,195.17	$49,053.79	**$103,248.96**
Pay period 21, October	$54,410.49	$49,344.01	**$103,754.50**
Pay period 22, October	$54,626.18	$48,058.80	**$102,684.98**
Pay period 23, November	$54,925.98	$46,751.96	**$101,677.94**
Pay period 24, November	$55,226.74	$43,312.50	**$98,539.24**
Pay period 25, December	$55,462.20	$42,232.37	**$97,694.57**
Pay period 26, December	$55,698.12	$44,281.35	**$99,979.47**

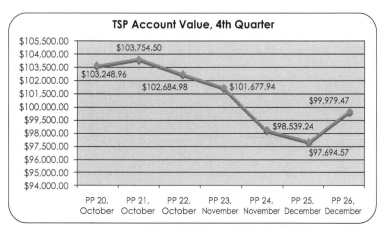

How do you feel?

At this point, ask yourself how you felt as your G Fund increased in value, while your C Fund decreased in value. Your $100,000 at the beginning of the year is now worth just $20 less and has an ending account balance of $99,979, even though one fund is up over 10% and one is down over 10%. What would your gut be telling you at this point, or at any point during the year?

1) Transfer the entire $44,000 from the C Fund—just under half of your total TSP account value—to the G Fund to protect what money you have left; adjust your biweekly contributions to have everything go to the G Fund.

2) Transfer a portion of the C Fund into the G Fund now to protect that money from possible further declines; adjust your biweekly contributions to put all of the $250 in the G Fund every two weeks as well.

3) Hold on to the $44,000 in the C Fund and hope that the market will go back up again, soon; continue to split the $250 in the C Fund and G Fund each pay period.

4) Following the adage to "buy low and sell high," transfer some money from the G Fund ("sell high") to the C Fund ("buy low") now that it is down, to even the two funds out and possibly increase investment returns 10 or 20 years from now. Increase biweekly contributions to invest each future $250 contribution into the C Fund as it continues to drop, to improve long-term investment results when the stock market finally recovers (even if it takes years).

As during Scenario 1 above, there is no "right" answer to these questions. It is important that you answer the questions honestly, because this type of market might recur in the future.

Entering year two, your TSP account recovers somewhat and by March it has again surpassed your original $100,000 account balance, reaching $101,000. Here is how your account performs through March:

	G Fund	**C Fund**	**Account Total**
Pay period 1, January	$55,848.19	$44,144.90	**$99,993.08**
Pay period 2, January	$55,998.32	$44,122.19	**$100,120.50**
Pay period 3, February	$56,221.31	$42,283.77	**$98,505.08**
Pay period 4, February	$56,444.70	$43,810.13	**$100,254.83**
Pay period 5, March	$55,971.39	$45,032.80	**$101,004.18**
Pay period 6, March	$55,503.09	$44,922.92	**$100,426.01**

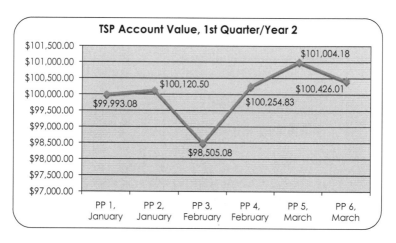

Your TSP account drops below $100,000 again in early spring. The main cause of the drop in value is the falling C Fund, which, by the end of May, plummets to below $41,000. Your G Fund, meanwhile, has increased to above $56,000. By the end of June in year two, you've added close to $10,000 of new money through biweekly contributions, but your TSP account total is just over $96,000 and still below your $100,000 balance 18 months ago. Here is how your TSP account performed through the end June of year two:

	G Fund	**C Fund**	**Account Total**
Pay period 7, April	$55,346.88	$43,080.49	**$98,427.37**
Pay period 8, April	$55,191.45	$43,548.24	**$98,739.69**
Pay period 9, April	$55,036.81	$42,530.54	**$97,567.35**
Pay period 10, May	$55,519.55	$41,220.62	**$96,740.17**
Pay period 11, May	$56,005.43	$40,911.03	**$96,916.46**
Pay period 12, June	$55,886.81	$42,920.33	**$98,807.14**
Pay period 13, June	$55,768.70	$40,553.79	**$96,322.49**

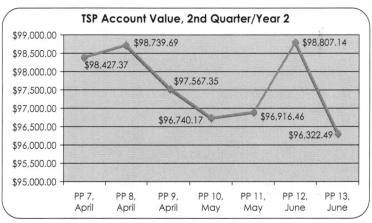

Through the summer months your account total drops further, and in late August, the account suffers the largest decline in the past two years as it falls to $90,431. A month later, in late September, your account balance drops below $90,000 for the first time in several years, to $88,568. By this time, you've contributed a total of $11,500 over the past 21 months, and what would have been at least $111,500 has now settled below $89,000, due entirely to a significant decline in the C Fund. Here is how your account balance looked through these months:

	G Fund	**C Fund**	**Account Total**
Pay period 14, July	$55,913.22	$39,334.86	**$95,248.07**
Pay period 15, July	$56,057.79	$39,105.06	**$95,162.85**
Pay period 16, August	$56,149.15	$38,499.22	**$94,648.37**
Pay period 17, August	$56,240.46	$34,191.52	**$90,431.98**
Pay period 18, September	$56,963.49	$34,254.40	**$91,217.88**
Pay period 19, September	$57,694.20	$33,765.49	**$91,459.68**
Pay period 20, September	$58,432.68	$30,135.56	**$88,568.24**

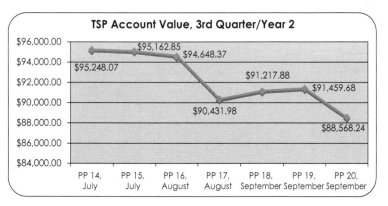

In October and November, your account balance recovers somewhat, however, as the C Fund increases by over 10% in value. Your TSP is now worth just over $95,000. While the C Fund continues to fluctuate between $33,000 and $35,000, your G Fund continues its steady climb upwards to over $62,000. Your total TSP account value hovers right above $95,000 through this time, however. Here is how your TSP account performed over these last few months of year two:

	G Fund	C Fund	Account Total
Pay period 21, October	$58,876.14	$35,065.62	**$93,941.75**
Pay period 22, October	$59,322.01	$35,966.83	**$95,288.84**
Pay period 23, November	$60,147.01	$35,132.78	**$95,279.79**
Pay period 24, November	$60,981.75	$34,309.97	**$95,291.71**
Pay period 25, December	$61,670.83	$33,012.94	**$94,683.77**
Pay period 26, December	$62,366.29	$33,172.40	**$95,538.68**

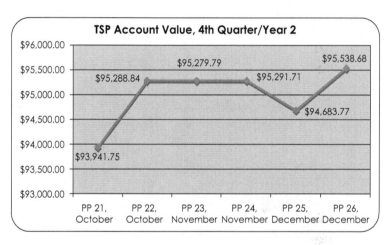

At the end of these two years, you would have about $95,500 in your TSP account had you invested 50% in the C Fund and 50% in the G Fund. This year-end amount includes the additional $250 contributions every two weeks—$125 to each fund—for total additional contributions of $13,000 over the past two years. While you have not experienced any growth over that time period, your total account is down a mere 4.45% from your original $100,000 over those two years, or just over 15% including your additional contributions over those two years.

Now, ask yourself the same questions as you asked yourself after Scenario 1. Which of the following decisions do you think you would make, or would have made at any time throughout the past year, as you watched your account during this scenario?

1) Transfer the entire $33,000 remaining in the C Fund—now just one-third of your total TSP account value, down from half two years ago—to the G Fund to protect what money you have left; adjust your biweekly contributions to have everything go to the G Fund.

2) Transfer a portion of the $33,000 remaining in the C Fund into the G Fund to protect it; adjust your biweekly contributions to put all of the $250 in the G Fund every two weeks as well.

3) Hold on to the $33,000 in the C Fund and hope that the market will go back up again soon; continue to split the $250 in the C Fund and G Fund each pay period.

4) Adhering to the maxim to "buy low and sell high," transfer some of your G Fund ("sell high") to the C Fund ("buy low"), following the considerable declines; change your biweekly contributions to put all of your new contributions into the C Fund.

Before discussing what type of investor you are based on how you answered the questions after scenarios 1 and 2 above, it is interesting to see how the S&P 500 performed—and how the C Fund would have performed—in the 20 years after this major "bear" market.

Looking at a chart of the S&P 500 over a 25-year period, from the beginning of 1970 to the end of 1994, this early-1970s period looks like a mere blip in the market. Indeed, there appear to be even steeper and more sudden declines in the late 1980s and early 1990s. Recall that in October 1987, the market dropped over 22% in one day! Yet, on a percentage basis, declines in the 1980s and early 1990s were less than the decline in 1973-1974.

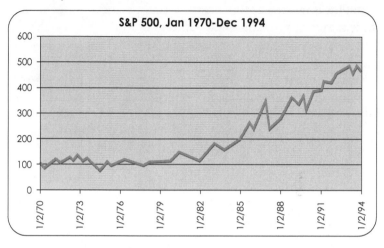

The 1973-1974 bear market looks like a small ripple when viewed over a 25-year period in the S&P 500 from 1970-1995.

Had you left your $69,000 untouched in the C Fund following Scenario 1 in 1974, your TSP account would have grown in line with the S&P 500 over the next 20 years, as seen in the above graph. Let's say you left government service at the end of this two-year period in Scenario 1, and you *did not make any further contributions* or otherwise touch your TSP account for another 20 years. From 1974 to 1994, the S&P 500 enjoyed significant double-digit returns, turning your $69,000 from Scenario 1 into over $1,050,000 at the end of 1994. Not bad for not adding a penny to it in those 20 years! In comparison, your $95,500 from Scenario 2 would have grown to just over $866,000 (with the G Fund growing to approximately $361,000 and the C Fund growing to $505,000 by the end of 1994), reflecting the relatively better returns in the S&P 500 compared to government bonds over those 20 years. And had you continued to add contributions during each pay period over those years, your TSP account in either of these scenarios would have increased considerably more.

This is not to say that every 20-year period will perform as well as 1975-1994. The stock market enjoyed a major bull market in the early 1980s through the 1990s, so this era was particularly good for long-term stock market investors. As noted previously, some 20-year periods will perform relatively more poorly for investors. But the examples above show that, even after steep declines in the stock market, the stock market can eventually recover and go higher if given enough time.

Your Investor Type

Based on your reactions to the two scenarios above, you can now categorize your tolerance for risk among the following investor types:

- If you answered 1 in the first scenario and 2 in the second scenario, you are a *conservative investor*.

- If you answered 2 or 3 in the first scenario and 2 or 3 in the second scenario, you are a *moderate investor*.

- If you answered 3 or 4 in the first scenario and answered 4 in the second scenario, you are an *aggressive investor*.

- Lastly, if you answered 1 following both scenarios, you are an *extremely conservative investor*. I would suggest reviewing the section on L Funds earlier in this Strategy and choosing an L Fund target year that matures no later than your early 50s.

Now that we've determined your interest in investing and your risk tolerance, Strategy II will provide sample TSP portfolio allocations based on your investor type.

STRATEGY II – ALLOCATE AMONG TSP FUNDS BASED ON YOUR TOLERANCE FOR RISK

One of the most difficult and confusing decisions to make when investing in the Thrift Savings Plan is how to allocate your investments among the TSP funds.

This is especially the case since the TSP funds can sometimes experience significant increases or decreases in value based on market conditions. When a given fund increases in value, the natural inclination is to add more money to the "winning" fund. At the same time, when a fund decreases in value, the natural inclination is to protect your remaining TSP investments by transferring money among the funds to the less volatile government bond fund.

But both of these inclinations are wrong. By strategically diversifying your TSP portfolio among the various funds based on pre-established parameters, you will be able to avoid selling when some TSP funds decline from time to time, and you will avoid overconfidence when some TSP funds increase significantly from time to time.

Diversification Among Asset Classes

In Strategy I, you saw how two different model portfolios performed during a severely declining market. In the first scenario, your $100,000 was fully invested in the C Fund, while in the second scenario you invested half your money in the C Fund and the other half in the G Fund. Over the two-year period in the exercise, the two-fund TSP portfolio performed much better than the one-fund portfolio. The two-fund portfolio suffered only minor declines, ending the period with close to $96,000, while the one-fund portfolio suffered significant declines and had approximately $69,000 by the end of the two-year period. At one point during the scenario, the one-fund portfolio was worth just $60,000!

Why the better performance in the two-fund portfolio? Because you *diversified* your account with funds from different asset classes. The C Fund, a growth-stock fund, did better during the go-go days of the 1960s, the 1980s, and the 1990s, while the G Fund, a safe bond fund, did relatively better as a refuge for investors during uncertain economic times in the 1970s, the early 1980s, and in the early 2000s. They performed differently under different market conditions.

The funds performed differently because they represent two different *asset classes*: The C Fund is a domestic U.S. large-capitalization stock asset class, while the G Fund is a U.S. Government bond asset class. Additionally, like the C Fund, the S and I Funds are both stock asset classes, but the S Fund is a domestic U.S. small-capitalization stock asset class, and the I

Fund is an international, large-capitalization stock asset class. While their performance will sometimes mimic the C Fund because they are both "stock" asset classes, some will perform better than others over time because of the different types of investments within this general stock asset class. The F Fund, in turn, is a U.S. total-bond asset class that includes U.S. Government debt, corporate debt, and asset-backed securities such as mortgage securities, which is a slightly different asset mix compared to the G Fund, which only invests in U.S. Treasury securities.

WHAT'S AN "ASSET?"

An "asset" is anything that retains value. Any asset that generally increases in value over time is considered an *appreciating asset*, while any asset that decreases in value over time is a *depreciating asset*. Your house is considered an appreciating asset because, in general, its value increases over time. Your car is a depreciating asset, because its value decreases over time (in fact, a car's value decreases as soon as you drive it off the dealer's lot, which is why cars should not be considered long-term investments).

Stocks, bonds, and real estate are generally appreciating assets, because they can increase in value for investors over time. Taken separately, they each can be considered an "asset class." Commodities—such as oil, natural gas, gold, silver, wheat, timber, etc.—make up a separate "asset class." Each of these asset classes tend to perform better at different times and under different market conditions, so when commodities or bonds are increasing in value as a group, stocks might fall, and when stocks as an asset class are increasing in value, bonds might decrease in value relative to stocks.

The TSP features two broad "asset classes": two bond funds (the G and F Funds) and three stock funds (the C, S, and I Funds). There has been some discussion in the past decade about adding new funds with different asset classes, such as a special real estate or a commodities fund, although these discussions never progressed beyond the very early stages. Whether such funds are ever added or not, it is important to remember that each of the stock funds includes companies that focus on real estate and commodities, so by investing in the TSP stock funds, you are investing a little in the real estate and the commodities sectors too, if indirectly. This—and the potential added cost and increased complexity of any new funds—are two reasons why new funds have not been added yet.

Finally, keep in mind that *you* are an asset as well. You are an asset to the government because of the value you bring each day in fulfilling your office's mission. Be sure to invest from time to time in your greatest assets of all by continuing your education and staying fit and healthy.

As you have probably observed by now, some TSP Funds do better than others in any given year. The chart below shows the best-returning and worst-returning TSP funds over ten years from 1998-2007.

	Best return...	**Worst return...**
2008	F Fund	S Fund
2007	I Fund	G Fund
2006	I Fund	F Fund
2005	I Fund	F Fund
2004	I Fund	G & F Fund (tied)
2003	S Fund	G & F Fund (tied)
2002	F Fund	C Fund
2001	F Fund	I Fund
2000	F Fund	S Fund
1999	S Fund	F Fund
1998	C Fund	G Fund

Source: Thrift Savings Plan website

Prior to this 10-year period, the C Fund enjoyed spectacular returns in the mid- and late-1990s, outperforming the S and I funds during those years. Because of its outsized returns in the 1990s, the C Fund did not perform as well as the S and I Funds in the mid-2000s.

The second-best returning fund in any given year over the past ten years was most often in the same asset class as the best-returning fund. When a stock fund enjoyed the best return that year, another stock fund had the second-best return, and when a bond fund had the best return for the year, the other bond fund came in second. In the 2000-2002 period, returns in the G Fund came a close second to the best-returning F Fund, while in 2003-2006 the S and C funds came in second and third place after the I Fund. The only year in which the second-best performing fund was in a different asset class during this 10-year period was in 2007, when the F Fund returned a few percentage points less than the I Fund.

Thus, as you can see, when a fund from one asset class performs best in any given year, often a fund from the other asset class comes in last for the year, and vice-versa. So in the late 1990s, funds from the stock asset class outperformed the bond asset class, while in 2000-2002 funds in the bond asset class outperformed funds in the stock asset class. In 2003-2006, funds in the stock asset class retook the lead, while 2007 appears to be a transition year, where stock asset class funds are losing momentum again to the bond asset class funds. Each of the stock funds suffered significant declines in 2008, while both of the bond funds enjoyed mid-single-digit returns.

While we would all want to be able to choose the best-returning fund—or even the best-returning asset class—in advance and invest all of our money in that fund until its performance begins to decline, this is impossible to do with any consistency. No one can know in advance which fund will perform better than all the others. You should never believe anyone who claims that he or she can maximize TSP returns by telling you in advance how to change your TSP allocation throughout the year, because he or she simply cannot know the future. Instead, the successful TSP investor will stick to a specific allocation among the funds based on investor type.

Just as we do not know which company will be the most successful and provide the best returns over time—hence the use of index funds to buy all the companies in any given stock market—we do not know what funds in the TSP will provide the best returns in any given year. While over very long periods of time stock funds (the C, S, and I funds) tend to provide better returns, during shorter periods of time they can also experience significant declines. The bond funds (the G and F funds) are more stable especially in volatile times and provide more income for older investors, but they do not grow as much over long periods of time. Therefore, it is best to invest in at least one fund of each asset class in the TSP. The TSP investor should invest a portion of his or her money in at least one bond fund (G or F Fund) and in at least one stock fund (C, I, or S Fund) for both growth in good times and balance during significant declines.

Thus, three sample portfolios emphasizing diversification among the asset classes are presented below based on your answers to the scenarios presented in Strategy I.

Strategic Portfolios for Risk-Conscious Investors

In Strategy I, we identified what type of investor you are based on your reaction to two scenarios featuring two different TSP portfolios—you are a *conservative investor*, a *moderate investor*, or an *aggressive investor*.

The conservative investor using the model portfolio below will experience less volatility during difficult markets. In return for the greater degree of safety, he or she will also probably experience a lower return over the very long term. The aggressive investor, on the other hand, might experience significant volatility, but as a result, will most likely experience a higher return compared to the conservative and moderate investors. The moderate investor will experience some volatility at times but also more growth over the very long term than the conservative investor.

By understanding these trade-offs in advance, you will be more likely to stick with your chosen investment strategy over the long term and will avoid selling your losing funds into declining markets or increasing your winning funds during times of over-exuberance.

 Portfolio for the Conservative Investor

For the conservative investor, a basic 50% allocation to stocks and a 50% allocation to bonds (similar to Scenario 2 in the previous chapter) will provide some growth while also protecting the total TSP account value during significant declines in stock markets.

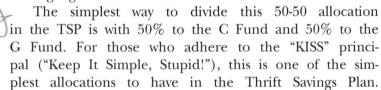 The simplest way to divide this 50-50 allocation in the TSP is with 50% to the C Fund and 50% to the G Fund. For those who adhere to the "KISS" principal ("Keep It Simple, Stupid!"), this is one of the simplest allocations to have in the Thrift Savings Plan.

While this basic allocation does not feature complete diversification among all the stock and bond asset classes, the C Fund contains at least some of the attributes of the S and I funds indirectly, providing more diversification in stocks than many realize. The C Fund includes a large majority of companies in the U.S. stock market (about 80% of all publicly traded companies), so you are getting some exposure to medium- and smaller-sized companies in addition to the largest U.S. companies that make up a significant portion of the C Fund. And many of these U.S.-based companies held in the C Fund have large global operations (think GE, Coca-Cola, and Boeing) earning significant profits from their overseas sales, providing some international exposure as well.

Basic Portfolio for Conservative Investors

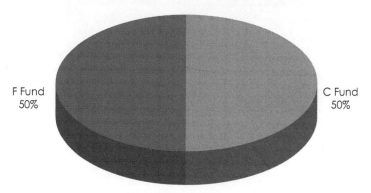

But for those conservative investors who would still like a slightly riskier allocation among the TSP funds, a basic 50-50 stock-to-bond ratio with the following model allocations provides some exposure to all the funds: 30% in the C Fund, 10% each in the S Fund and I Fund, and 20-30% in the F Fund with the remainder in the G Fund. The addition of the small-cap and international funds provides a little more potential growth—and a little more risk—while maintaining an overall less-risky 50-50 stock-to-bond allocation. The F Fund, in turn, includes a significant amount of corporate and other asset-backed bonds in addition to U.S. Government bonds, thus expanding beyond the basic G Fund government bond holdings

These allocations can fluctuate 5% in either direction, based on personal preferences.

Diversified Portfolio for Conservative Investors

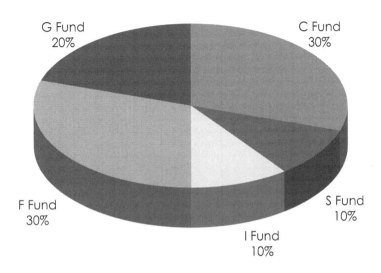

Portfolio for the Moderate Investor

For the moderate investor, a 60% total allocation to stocks and a 40% total allocation to bonds provides a little more opportunity for growth while still protecting the total TSP value from significant swings in the market. This might be the preferred portfolio for a majority of risk-conscious investors, as the 60% in stocks allows for a little extra growth over time, while the 40% allocation to bonds protects investors from most kinds of downturns investors can expect to experience in U.S. and international equities markets. Moreover, this leaves a significant cushion to use to invest during periodic downturns in the stock funds, as will be discussed in Strategies III and IV.

The simplest way to diversify a moderate portfolio is to invest 60% in the C Fund and 40% in the G Fund, similar to the "KISS" allocation strategy above. For those who wish to further diversify their 60% stock allocation, 35% of the total portfolio could be invested the C Fund, 15% in the I Fund, and 10% in the S Fund. For the bond allocation, 20% could be invested each in the F and G Funds, give or take 5-10% among the funds.

Diversified Portfolio for Moderate Investors

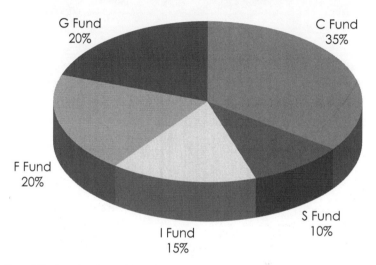

Portfolio for the Aggressive Investor

For the aggressive investor who is seeking the greater potential long-term growth and is comfortable with some-times-significant volatility—and declines—from time to time in their portfolios, an allocation of 70% to stocks and the remainder in bonds provides growth potential while also leaving a significant cushion for investing during declining markets, as discussed in Strategy IV. Forty per-cent invested in the C Fund, 20% in the I Fund, and 10% in the S Fund, with 15% each in the G and F Funds yields a fully diversified portfolio, with 5-10% difference in allo-cations among the funds based on personal preference.

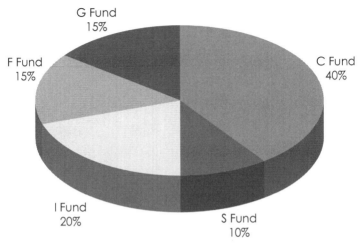

Diversified Portfolio for Aggressive Investors

G Fund 15%
F Fund 15%
C Fund 40%
I Fund 20%
S Fund 10%

The observant reader has by now realized that even this "aggressive investor" TSP allocation puts relatively less in the TSP stock funds than some of the longer-term L Funds. For example, the aggressive allocation above would, in 2015, have 5% less invested in stocks than the L 2040 Fund, with a 75-25 stock-bond allocation.

The lower stock-bond allocations in the conservative and moderate investor strategies are designed to protect against undue fluctuations in one's TSP total account value during times of significant market swings, as noted previously.

The increased bond allocation in the aggressive portfolio is also intended to leave significant resources to buy into declining markets, as occurred in 1973-74, 1987, 2000-02, and in 2008-09, to "supercharge" one's investments. These strategies are detailed more fully in the next two chapters.

I would not recommend a 100% allocation to the stock funds even for those who want maximum risk for what

they believe will be maximum return, because to
mean we would have to forgo significant inves
tunities during severe downturns in the marke
extra pool of funds readily available in the G and F Funds,
the aggressive investor can use the markets' volatility to his
or her advantage, drawing from these funds to invest in the
other declining funds.

The bond portion of the aggressive investor's TSP
account—the G and F Funds—will fluctuate to a greater
extent depending on market conditions so that, as buying
opportunities emerge during declines in the stock markets, the bond portion of this total allocation will decrease.
In Strategy IV, the aggressive investor will watch for specific buying opportunities during market declines, and, in
so doing, bond allocations might drop from 30% to 15%,
10%, or to even less. Once the stock markets recover, the
aggressive investor will then employ Strategy III to build
the bond portfolio slowly back up to 20% or 30%, in
order to repeat the process as necessary during future
market swings. The aggressive portfolio will therefore be
the most dynamic among the three portfolios outlined
above when employing both Strategy III and Strategy IV.

Summary for Strategy II

The TSP investor should allocate his or her investments among the stock and bond funds based on risk
tolerance identified in Strategy I.

- If you are a *conservative investor*, allocate 50% of
  your portfolio to the stock funds (C, S, and I) and
  50% to the bond funds (G and F). Rebalance your
  TSP account over time according to Strategy III,
  and consider recommendations in Strategy V.

- If you are a *moderate investor*, allocate 60% of your portfolio among the stock funds and 40% among the bond funds. Rebalance your TSP account over time according to Strategy III, and consider recommendations in Strategy V. (The more adventurous moderate investor might also want to consider Strategy IV, with the understanding that this strategy entails greater fluctuations in one's total TSP allocation strategy.)

- If you are an *aggressive investor*, allocate 70% of your portfolio among the stock funds and 30% among the bond funds. This investor will also be the most active when employing Strategies III and IV. Also consider the recommendations in Strategy V.

STRATEGY III – REBALANCE YOUR FUNDS WITH THE HELP OF BIWEEKLY OR MONTHLY CONTRIBUTIONS

Once you have established a target allocation among the TSP funds based on your investor type, it is useful to know how to rebalance your holdings among the funds, since your total allocation to the different funds will change naturally over time.

When investing in several different TSP funds with different average growth rates, some of the funds will naturally increase in value faster than others. This is called *portfolio drift*, or the slow change over time from a targeted allocation (for example, from the moderate investor's 60-40 allocation) to one reflecting recent market conditions.

Under historically average market conditions, the stock funds should grow at their historical average of about 9-10% per year, and the bond funds should grow at their historical rate of about 5-6% per year. Even within the first year under these average market conditions, the stock funds will represent a slightly greater proportion of your TSP account, because the total investment in the stock funds will grow more than the investment in the bond funds.

If the stock funds enjoy a few years of outsized growth—such as in the late 1990s, when the C Fund grew by over 20% each year for five years—they will increase in value disproportionately compared to the bond funds. Conversely, during significant declines in the U.S. and world stock markets, the stock funds will contract quickly relative to the bond funds.

Thus, when U.S. and world stock markets are performing well, your TSP holdings might change from a 60-40 or 70-30 allocation between stock and bond funds to 65-35 or 75-25 allocation or greater within a few years. While the increase in value of the stock funds over the bond funds might make you feel wealthier, this also means that an unexpected stock market correction or significant decline in U.S. and world stock markets will cause a greater proportion of your portfolio (i.e., your stock funds) to decrease quickly in value as a result. Several years of portfolio drift will create a disproportionate allocation between your stock and bond funds, and as a result more of your TSP is at greater risk during any future market declines.

Therefore, from time to time the TSP investor will want to readjust or rebalance his or her fund holdings back to the original allocation to remain aligned with one's investor type. Rebalancing during significant increases in a given fund or funds also forces the TSP investor to focus on investing more in the relatively cheaper funds, as they represent better values in relation to the other funds.

Portfolio Drift and Periodic Rebalancing

Within the TSP—as within many long-term periodic investment programs—reallocation among the funds can be accomplished through two methods.

The first method is the traditional rebalancing of one's total holdings at one time using an interfund transfer. In this method, you shift some money from those funds that have grown beyond their initial target allocations to funds that have fallen below their initial target allocations in one transaction.

This simple method can be accomplished at any time during the year, and the transaction can be completed in one or two business days. However, because TSP investors are also usually investing in the same funds every pay period via biweekly or monthly contributions, TSP investors are in effect re-investing new money in those funds almost immediately after rebalancing via the interfund transfer, partially offsetting the effect of the transfer.

For example, a moderate investor with a 60-40 stock-bond allocation experiences portfolio drift, so that he now has 63% of his money in the C Fund and 37% in the F Fund. He chooses to readjust his fund holdings by interfund transfer, moving that extra 3% from the C Fund to the F Fund in one transaction. However, if this investor is also splitting his biweekly contributions along the same 60-40 allocation, then his interfund transfer—selling from the C Fund to transfer money to the F Fund—is, within weeks, partially offset by new money contributed to the C Fund. This investor is re-investing money into a fund that he just transferred money out of.

Thus, under normal market conditions, rebalancing and then re-investing in those same rebalanced funds with biweekly contributions can be a wasted activity.

The second method instead uses biweekly contributions to rebalance one's TSP funds, by allocating all new biweekly contributions to the underweighted funds until they have reached their target allocations. Of course, this method can take more time—several months or more—to accomplish. While this method requires some patience, it has the benefit of avoiding the unnecessary shifting of already invested money between any of the TSP funds. You can truly remain a "buy and hold" investor using this method.

Before more fully illustrating how these two methods work, let's first take a look at how portfolio drift might impact model TSP allocations.

Drifting TSP Funds

As an example of how an investor's portfolio can naturally change or "drift" from a target allocation, the below example portfolio shows a mid-career moderate investor with $100,000 in her TSP account that experiences significant growth in the stock funds relative to the bond funds.

Isabella Jones, a 12-year employee of the Department of Energy, has $100,000 in her TSP. As a moderate investor, she has allocated her portfolio among all the funds as described in Strategy II—$35,000 in her large-cap C fund, $15,000 and $10,000 respectively in the I and S funds, $20,000 in the G fund, and another $20,000 in her F fund. In total, Isabella has 60% of her portfolio in the stock funds and 40% in the bond funds. She was recently promoted to GS-13 and makes about $70,000 a year. She contributes 14% of her pay to the TSP, and with the government match, she invests just over $500 every two weeks to her TSP.

Isabella enjoys a year of significant growth in her stock funds, with the C fund growing approximately 15% and the I and S funds growing close to 20% each in one year. Her bond funds enjoy steady returns as well, with the G and F funds growing at 4% and 6%, respectively. This growth, in addition to her $13,000 worth of contributions, brings her total TSP holdings to just over $126,000. This also means, however, that Isabella's 60-40 stock-bond allocation has drifted to over 62-38, reflecting the greater growth in her stock funds (see below).

	Beginning balance	TSP Fund Allocation	End balance	TSP Allocati
G Fund	$20,000.00	20%	$23,504.00	19%
F Fund	$20,000.00	20%	$23,956.00	19%
C Fund	$35,000.00	35%	$45,482.50	36%
I Fund	$15,000.00	15%	$20,001.00	16%
S Fund	$10,000.00	10%	$13,334.00	11%
Total	$100,000.00		$126,277.50	

If Isabella's stock funds continue to enjoy increased growth over several years, her allocation would drift even further away from her chosen 60-40 allocation.

Now, Isabella has the option to rebalance her funds back to her desired TSP allocation, at any time, using the interfund transfer on the TSP website. On the "inter-fund transfer" page, Isabella would see the dollar amount in each of her funds and the total percentage this repre-sents in her TSP portfolio—approximately 19% in the G Fund, 19% in the F Fund, 36% in the C Fund, 16% in the I Fund, and 16% in the S Fund. Next to each of these per-centages, Isabella would fill in her original target allocation percentages for each fund for a moderate investor (20-20-35-15-10, respectively). After providing her email address to receive final confirmation of the interfund transfer and re-confirming her interfund transfer request, the whole process is done. About two days later, Isabella receives an e-mail from TSP confirming that the transaction took place.

TSP investors can use this reallocation method to rebalance among the funds at predetermined times during the year—every three months, for example, or at the end of each year. Alternatively, investors can rebalance once their accounts have drifted beyond a certain percentage in fund holdings—for

e funds have drifted 5% above or below
Rebalancing via an interfund transfer
undertaken too often; there is no need
tly the set percentages, since some drift
both directions on any given trading
day. Also, the TSP administrators limits interfund transfers
to a maximum of two in any given month, so more active
TSP investors will have to keep these limits in mind, as well.

For buy-and-hold investors, interfund transfers are somewhat of an unsatisfying exercise. As noted above, by using an
interfund transfer to reallocate your investments all at once,
you are essentially selling shares from some TSP funds to rebalance the amounts in the remaining funds. But because most
TSP investors are also investing in those funds via periodic
contributions, an investor would invest new money again in
those same funds within weeks of rebalancing, assuming the
investor's contributions mirrors his or her total allocation.

Let's take a look again at Isabella's portfolio to illustrate
the reallocation process more closely. By rebalancing, Isabella had to sell around $1,000 each from her C/S/I Funds
to add $1,700 and $1,300 to the G and F Funds respectively.

	Before Rebalancing	**After Rebalancing**
G Fund	$23,504.00	$25,255.50
F Fund	$23,956.00	$25,255.50
C Fund	$45,482.50	$44,197.13
I Fund	$20,001.00	$18,941.63
S Fund	$13,334.00	$12,627.75
Total	**$126,277.50**	**$126,277.50**

If Isabella's biweekly contribution allocation is the same as
her TSP account's total contribution, she would be investing
around $175 into the C Fund, $75 into the I Fund, $50 into

the S Fund, and $100 each into the G and F Funds every two weeks, continuing as she rebalanced. Within 10 pay periods— four or five months—Isabella would have thus re-invested the same amount into each of the C/S/I Funds as she had sold during her interfund transfer. The biweekly contributions in effect negated some of the rebalancing activity, as Isabella ended up re-investing in the same funds she sold out of (the C, I, and S Funds) to rebalance into the bond funds (the G and F Funds) within weeks of conducting the interfund transfer.

Why sell something just to turn around and buy it back again?

Rebalancing Via Biweekly Contributions

Under normal market conditions, there is another method to rebalance one's TSP holdings that does not require TSP investors to shift any money from the growing funds to rebalance the remaining funds. Instead of rebalancing via an interfund transfer, you can invest in the underweighted funds via biweekly contributions.

Rebalancing via biweekly contributions takes more time and patience to complete, but it has the advantage of avoiding the sale of any investments in any of the funds. You can remain a "buy and hold," long-term investor. Using this method, you are just investing new money in the underweighted funds, instead of selling shares from the funds that have enjoyed significant growth.

Let's take a look again at Isabella's situation to see how this would work. Isabella, a buy-and-hold TSP investor, does not want to shift money out of any of her stock funds— they've gained so much already, after all—and she instead wants to let her stock-fund holdings continue to grow. Therefore, she will simply add money to her unbalanced bond funds using her biweekly $500+ investments, until she has reached her desired allocation of 60-40 once again.

To do this, Isabella changes her $500 biweekly contributions to go entirely to the bond funds—50% F Fund and 50% G Fund, or about $250 each into the G and F funds. To accomplish this, Isabella would access the "biweekly contribution" page in her TSP account (instead of the "interfund transfer" page) and would enter 50% each in the G and F Funds. Once she enters her e-mail address and confirms the transaction, the TSP administrators will send her a message within several days confirming the change. Isabella will not add any new money to the three stock funds until her bond funds have re-attained their 40% target allocation—her bond allocation as a moderate investor.

Because she continues to invest a significant amount in her TSP account via biweekly contributions, in just six pay periods (or three months) Isabella would have added a total of $3,000 to the G and F Funds, thus increasing their values in a relatively short amount of time. Assuming no major increases in the stock funds, because her TSP total value has increased due to the additional $3,000 in contributions, Isabella would want to contribute a few more pay periods to the bond funds to fully attain the 60-40 balance. And, if her stock funds continued to enjoy significant returns, Isabella can continue to add to the G and F Funds to fully re-balance her TSP account even as her stock funds continue to grow.

Once Isabella was satisfied with her total allocation, she could change her biweekly contribution again to reflect her original allocation preference, with 60% of her biweekly contributions going into her stock funds and 40% going into her bond funds. Alternatively, in anticipation of further long-term growth in her stock funds, Isabella could set her biweekly contributions to add a little more to her bond funds, relative to her stock funds—say, 25% or even

30% of her $500 biweekly contributions each to the G and F funds, with the remainder going to the stock funds.

Importantly, this process can be reversed during significant declines in the stock markets as well. Let's say Isabella's stock portfolio suddenly *declined* 10% or 15%, thus slightly over-weighting her bond funds relative to her stock funds. She could then increase her biweekly contributions to invest more into her stock funds, thus investing into these funds as the stock market declines and as stocks become progressively cheaper.

Moreover, this technique does not violate the TSP's policy against frequent trading, so aggressive investors will retain their two interfund transfers per month to use during significant down markets, as will be discussed in Strategy IV.

The Art of Rebalancing Over Time

For this method to be effective, the TSP investor must first be contributing a healthy percentage of pay via biweekly contributions. A contribution of just a few percent of pay every two weeks is probably not enough to rebalance one's TSP holdings. If Isabella were contributing 4% of her pay instead of 14%, her biweekly contributions would drop to under $250, effectively doubling the time it would take to rebalance the stock and bond funds in her TSP account. Biweekly contributions of 10% or even 15% substantially improve the success of this Strategy (and add more quickly to one's TSP account, too!).

Also, as one's TSP account grows over time, rebalancing via biweekly contributions will naturally take longer to accomplish. If, instead of $100,000, Isabella had $300,000 in her account, it would take her much longer to rebalance her funds with her $500 biweekly contributions. Her $300,000 would have grown to almost $350,000 at the end of the year, with close to $131,500 in the two bond funds and over $218,000 in the stock funds (see table). To regain her 60-40 allocation,

Isabella would have to increase her bond fund holdings to $140,000. With a $500 biweekly contribution, it would take around 17 pay periods—about nine months—to add an additional $8,500 to her bond funds, assuming marginal growth in her stock funds.* It would take even longer if Isabella's stock funds continued to enjoy significant growth over that time.

	Beginning balance	TSP Fund Allocation	End balance	TSP Fund Allocation
G Fund	$60,000	20%	$65,104.00	18.61%
F Fund	$60,000	20%	$66,356.00	18.97%
C Fund	$105,000	35%	$125,982.50	36.01%
I Fund	$45,000	15%	$55,401.00	15.84%
S Fund	$30,000	10%	$36,934.00	10.56%
Total	**$300,000**		**$349,777.50**	

Moreover, one's TSP account could fluctuate greatly during times of significant market volatility, causing significant portfolio drift in a short period of time. If Isabella's stock funds experienced a drop of 30% in the following year, her $218,000 would have declined in value to $152,600, and now her TSP account would be close to 54-46 stock-bonds, thus overweighting her bond funds relative to the stock funds for the moderate investor. Isabella here would allocate all

---

* Note that Isabella's biweekly contributions slowly increase the total amount in her TSP account and, as a result, increase the target amount to achieve the 40% allocation for the bond funds. With close to $350,000 in her TSP in this example, Isabella would have to increase her bond allocation from $131,500 to $140,000 to achieve the 40% allocation. But by adding $8,500, her TSP total increases to $358,000, which means Isabella's 40% bond allocation target is now $143,200, requiring a few more contributions to the bond funds to fully rebalance. In reality, all the funds will fluctuate every day, making exact target allocations unrealistic, however.

of her biweekly contributions to the stock funds to invest into the rapidly declining stock markets. Given the severity and rapid nature of the declines, Isabella could additionally request an interfund transfer to shift a few percentage points from her bond funds to her stock funds, to bring it back to a 57-43 or 58-42 stock-bond allocation, even as she continues to invest her biweekly contributions into the stock funds to gradually regain her 60-40 target allocation.

Thus, rebalancing via biweekly or monthly contributions becomes more of an art than a science, as your TSP account total value grows and as you encounter significant volatility in the markets from time to time. If your preferred target allocation has drifted 5-10% in one direction even after allocating biweekly contributions into the underweight funds, an interfund transfer of a few percentage points might be necessary to regain a more optimal allocation. One should reallocate only a few percentage points at a time via the interfund transfer, however, in anticipation of further volatility in the markets—a sudden recovery in the value of the falling funds, for example.

Strategy IV will further discuss how to invest into significantly declining markets and is primarily intended for aggressive investors. Conservative and moderate investors who are comfortable with their investment allocation and rebalancing strategies to this point can skip to Strategy V.

Summary for Strategy III

- Review your TSP account periodically—quarterly or twice yearly—to ensure your TSP funds are allocated according to your investor type.

- Under normal market conditions, if your TSP funds are more than a few percentage points different than their target allocations, rebalance the funds slowly over time by allocating your periodic contributions to the underweighted funds. To ensure greater success with this method, contribute an adequate percentage of your base pay—10% to 15%—via your biweekly or monthly contributions.

- During times of significant market volatility, when the allocation of one or more of your funds has drifted by more than five percentage points from your target allocation, reallocate a few percent via the interfund transfer, in addition to biweekly contributions to the underweighted funds.

STRATEGY IV – SUPERCHARGE YOUR TSP BY INVESTING AS FUNDS FALL

To achieve truly significant growth in wealth over time, TSP stock fund investors should be prepared to invest into significant market declines at predetermined intervals, when stock funds become increasingly cheaper.

However, as illustrated in Scenarios 1 and 2 in Strategy I, having a significant portion of one's portfolio invested in the TSP stock funds when stock markets decline will cause commensurate declines in one's total TSP account value as well. This is why Strategy IV is recommended *only* for those with an appetite for risk. Only those who can withstand significant declines in their TSP account over potentially long periods of time (from several months to several years or longer) should consider using this strategy.

Yet, the rewards of investing into stock funds as they decline can be quite significant over several decades. Peter Lynch illustrated the long-term benefits of buying into major market declines in his 1993 classic *Beating the Street*. Lynch commissioned research that found that $1,000 invested in the S&P 500 index on January 31 each year from 1940 to 1992 would have grown to just over $3.5 million after 52 years and a total investment of $52,000. This equates to a 12% average yearly return, which is very good. But by adding $1,000 each time the market dropped 10% or more—which happened 31 times over those 52 years (on average about once every 20 months) according to Lynch—the investor's $83,000 total investment would have been worth over $6.2 million by the end of 1992.[28] The extra $31,000 invested during market downturns ultimately grew an additional *$2.7 million* in this scenario!

Of course, stock prices were extremely low in the 1940s, after the Great Depression and during World War II, so that any investment in the stock market then would have enjoyed significant gains over 50 years later. However, while returns will differ depending on when one starts investing, the technique can be applied at any time; by investing a little extra when the stock market declines at predetermined percentage intervals, an investor will see greater gains over the long term than if he or she just continued to invest the same amount among the funds each year.

Let's recalculate this same $1,000 yearly investment over a more reasonable time period, from 1970 to 2010. Forty years is a more realistic time frame to consider since a 20- or 25-year-old might invest in stocks until he or she is 60 or 65 and then choose to enjoy his or her wealth thereafter. It should be noted that 1970-2010 also includes steep market declines in 1973-1974, 1987, 2000-2002, and 2008-2009, so that any investment would have experienced significant fluctuations.

By investing $1,000 in the S&P 500 at the beginning of 1970, and investing the same amount at the beginning of each year through 2010—$40,000 in total—the stock investor would have approximately $616,000 by the end of 2010. Not quite the millions of dollars as in Lynch's example, but a significant return on a $40,000 total investment over the years nevertheless. (And this is yet another example of the potential long-term returns of the stock market!)

Further, by investing an additional $1,000 in the January after each year that experienced a decline of 8% or more at the end of the calendar year (six times in total), the stock investor would have turned a $46,000 investment over 40 years into over $718,000. The addition of a mere $6,000 following significant market declines added over $100,000 to the investor's account! And these additional $1,000 investments do not include times when the stock market declined 10% or more but then recovered within the same calendar year, such as in October 1987. Investing on those occasions as well would have yielded even more sizeable gains at the end of a 40-year investing career (see appendix for year-by-year calculations).

Moreover, a majority of TSP investors can likely contribute more than $1,000 per year into TSP stock funds and other investments. Imagine what the result might be if, instead of investing $1,000 per year, you invest $5,000, $10,000, or even $15,000 per year. The results are likely to be spectacular, as long as you have the patience and fortitude to withstand the declines over time and have a stable reserve of funds from which to invest into stock funds during market declines.

To illustrate this, instead of investing $1,000 each year for 40 years, what would the value have been at the end of 2010 had an investor increased contributions by 5% each year? A 5% yearly increase would gradually increase an investor's yearly contribution from $1,000 in 1970 to $7,040 by 2010, with total contributions from 1970 to 2010 reaching $127,840 over a 40-year period. One's TSP account, however, would be worth over $994,000 by the end of 2010—over 50% greater than by just investing a constant $1,000 each year. And by doubling the contribution following years experiencing significant declines, one's total investment would be worth over $1,145,000—$150,000 more even than just investing an increasing amount each year. (See Appendix for yearly returns of each type of investment.)

How would you like to leave a career in government service with a nest egg approaching $1 million or more? As the above examples indicate, steady investments over long time periods with additional investments during significant stock market declines can yield outsized gains.

Yet, seemingly unaware that investing during stock market declines can provide significant returns over the long run, many individual investors do not invest during these times of market volatility. In fact, some TSP investors do the *opposite* of this and sell into declines in the mistaken belief that this will protect their remaining savings from further losses. As Warren Buffet wrote in his 1997 Annual Report to shareholders, "many investors" who are "going to be net buyers of stocks for many years to come"—five years or more—"are elated when stock prices rise and depressed when they fall." But "[t]his reaction makes no sense," as long-term investors "*should much prefer sinking prices*" (my emphasis added).[29] When prices go down, the stock investor can invest more cheaply and enjoy greater returns in the long run. And in a later report, Buffet explained that if investors "insist on trying to time their participation in equities, they should try to be fearful when others are greedy and greedy when others are fearful."[30] "Greedy investors" (I prefer the term "aggressive investors") are prepared to invest when the market presents a good, long-term value following a significant decline.

The trick is to know how to buy into declining markets.

Supercharge Your TSP: Buy Into Falling Stock Funds Based on Percentage Declines

For TSP investors, buying into declining markets is relatively simple to do.

According to Strategy II, aggressive investors should keep 30% of their TSP portfolio in the bond funds—with at least half of that amount in the G Fund—during normal market conditions. The rest is invested among the stock funds.

As an aggressive investor, once you have allocated your TSP account holdings among the funds, keep track of the TSP funds' performance. Your time to buy will come when any of the three stock funds falls at least 10% from its most recent high. Once this happens, transfer 1% of your total holdings from the G Fund into the fund that has just fallen 10% or more.

Because they are a similar asset class, the three stock funds often rise or decline in tandem, although not always to the same degree. When one stock fund has declined, the others are likely to have declined to some extent as well. When this is the case, simply round the other stock funds up to the next whole percentage when conducting the interfund transfer to add a little extra money to them, in addition to adding a full percentage point to the fund that has fallen by 10% (see following example). Again, most of this should come from the G Fund, and the F Fund should be rounded down to the next lowest percentage point in the process.

Continue to watch the TSP stock funds' performance. The next buying opportunity will come when the same stock fund or funds have dropped an additional 10%. Once this happens, repeat the process by using the interfund transfer to move another 1% of your portfolio from the G Fund into the fallen stock fund(s). Repeat this process if the fund(s) drop another 10%, and so on.

Your G Fund might be depleted after investing into four or five 10% downturns, or when at least one of the stock funds have dropped a total of 40% or more. If this is the case, you can now draw from the F Fund to invest into the next 10% stock fund decline. Indeed, the value of the F Fund might have actually *increased* during this time, as other panicking investors are increasingly seeking out safe havens such as bonds and bond funds for their investments, thus increasing the value of bonds relative to stocks. This is to your advantage if this happens, as you are using a fund that has increased in value (the F Fund) to buy into a stock fund or funds that are now cheaper and, as a result, represent better values.

This is the ultimate exercise of the adage to "buy low, sell high"—you are selling the F Fund that has likely increased in value ("sell high"), and you are investing into stock funds that have fallen in value ("buy low").

By initially keeping 30% of your TSP investments in the G and F Funds under normal market conditions, you will have enough reserves available to invest at 10% increments through at least a 50% drop—five separate times—in all three stock funds. The aggressive investor also has enough of a cushion remaining to invest a final amount should the market decline a total of 60% or more. Maintain discipline during the declines and only invest once during each 10% decline to retain some resources in reserve for the next decline, if necessary. If one fund drops below its 10% decline target and you perform an interfund transfer—while the other stock funds have dropped only 8%, for example—there is probably no need to perform another transfer of funds if a second stock fund drops below its 10% decline target a few weeks later. If the trend continues, and one of these funds drops another full 10%, you can of course conduct another interfund transfer into each of these declining funds at that point.

Remember also that, according to current TSP policy, TSP investors can only perform two interfund transfers a month into the stock funds, so be judicious in conducting these transfers during especially volatile markets. The TSP investor can also employ Strategy III during market declines to add new contributions to declining funds, as well.

Strategy IV in Action

Let's look at recent TSP fund share price moves from late 2007 through 2010 to see how this strategy would work.

In October 2007, the C, S, and I stock index funds hit their highs around the same time as U.S. and international stock markets were experiencing significant increases in value. On October 9, the C Fund hit its all-time high of $17.57 per share, while the S Fund hit its all-time high of $21.29 the next day. Around that time, the I Fund hit an all-time high of $25.73, but on October 31, it reached another high of $26.31 per share.*

In planning potential buy targets if a downturn were to take place, the price target for each of these funds following a 10% fall from these highs would be $15.81 for the C Fund, $19.16 for the S Fund, and $23.68 for the I Fund. The price target to buy after a 20% fall would be $14.06, $17.03, and $21.05 respectively (see chart below).

	October 2007 high	Decline of 10%	Decline of 20%	Decline of 30%	Decline of 40%	Decline of 50%
C Fund	$17.57	$15.81	$14.06	$12.30	$10.54	$8.79
S Fund	$21.29	$19.16	$17.03	$14.90	$12.77	$10.65
I Fund	$26.31	$23.68	$21.05	$18.47	$15.79	$13.16

Following the October 2007 highs, the markets began to fall the following month. All three funds approached their 10% buy targets by late November 2007, but before falling below their

---

* Since the stock funds had hit all-time highs the previous summer and fall and most likely would have increased your stock-to-bond allocation beyond the 70-30 proposed for aggressive investors, the aggressive investor following Strategy III would have been adding new contributions to G Fund and F Fund holdings to slowly rebalance them back to their 30% allocation. Thus, not only would the aggressive investor have more in the bond funds to invest during the coming market downturn, he or she would have avoided investing new contributions at a major stock market peak in the fall of 2007 by following Strategy III.

respective thresholds, each gained a few percentage points within the next few weeks. Only the S Fund fell briefly below its 10% decline buy target, to $19.05 on November 21, while the other two funds recovered somewhat before the end of 2007.

Yet the declines continued into the new year. In January, the S Fund was the first to fall below its 10% target (again), falling to $18.80 a share on January 4, and it continued to decline thereafter. The C Fund fell below its 10% price target a few days later, falling on January 8 to $15.69, although it recovered to $15.90 the following day. The I Fund flirted with a full 10% drop at the same time, falling to $23.88 that week, only to rise again in the following days. The bond funds, meanwhile, actually increased slightly during this time, with the F Fund increasing from $11.59 to $12.08 per share by January 11.

Since one fund dropped convincingly below its 10% decline target in early January and the other two funds dropped close to their respective 10% decline targets around this time as well, this would have been a good time to add some money to these funds via an interfund transfer. For the fund that dropped below its 10% decline target, increase it by one percentage point and round up to the next percentage point. The investor would do this also for the funds that were very near their 10% decline targets. For the funds that have dropped but have not yet dipped below their 10% decline target, simply round up to the next highest percentage point when conducting the interfund transfer. Decrease the allocation by this same percentage from the G Fund, and round the F Fund down to the next whole percentage point.

Stock markets sometimes recover quickly following a 10% decline—which is sometimes called a "correction"—but this did not happen in early 2008. U.S. and international equities markets instead continued to fall. Following another rapid sell-off in March, by July 2008 all major indexes had crossed into bear-market territory, defined as a decline of 20% or more.

The C Fund dropped to $14.01 on July 14, below the 20% decline threshold of $14.06. The next day, the C Fund dropped again to $13.86, indicating that the fund was solidly in bear territory. On this day also, the I Fund dropped to $20.67, well below its 20% decline level of $21.05. Thus, it too had dropped into bear market territory.

The C and I Funds' additional 10% decline provided another buy signal. Thus, one would simply repeat the process above: increase the C and I Funds by a full percentage point and round up to the next full number via an interfund transfer. The S Fund dropped to $17.23, not quite to its 20% decline level of $17.03 but close enough to warrant adding a percentage point to this fund as well.

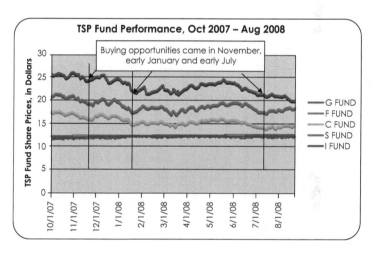

You would have shifted around 6% or 7% of your portfolio from the bond funds to the stock funds by this point, and would have enough for at least four more interfund transfers into each of the stock funds should they decline further.

In fact, more buying opportunities emerged in late 2008 and early 2009, as the economic crisis deepened. On September 28, the I Fund dropped to $17.42, a drop of 30% from its high in 2007. Within a week, the C Fund share price dropped to $12.12 on October 6, while the S Fund dropped to $14.51, down over 30% from their respective 2007 highs. The I Fund dropped again the next day to $15.56, representing a fall of 40% from its high a year before. The C Fund and S Fund fell again to $10.44 and $12.43 two days later, now down 40% from their respective highs the previous year, thus presenting yet another buy signal.

The steep market declines continued into the new year. In mid-January 2009, the I Fund dropped to $13.02, now down 50%, although the C Fund and S Fund did not reach these levels until mid-February, when they fell to $8.63 and $10.43, respectively, on February 20. The stock markets bottomed on March 9, 2009, with the C Fund dropping to $7.87, the S Fund to $9.06, and the I Fund to $10.29.

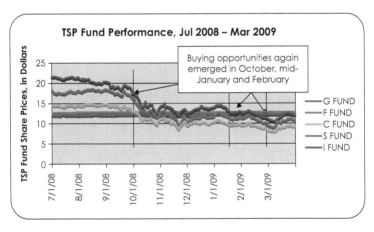

Even as these funds fall, the aggressive investor should plan for an eventual recovery. Once the markets have regained 50% from their absolute bottoms—or have regained their losses and have reached new highs (depending on the severity of the downturn)—it is time to rebuild your G Fund and F Fund holdings in preparation for eventual future market declines. Do this by changing your biweekly contributions to a 50-50 G Fund-F Fund allocation (or 100% to the G Fund, if you are using that as your primary bond fund in the 70-30 allocation strategy), as noted in Strategy III.

The stock funds began a steady recovery in spring 2009 through early 2010. In just over a year, the TSP stock funds had nearly doubled from their March 2009 lows, with the C Fund rising to $14.45, the S Fund to $19.48, and the I Fund to $18.89 by late-April 2010.

One final buying opportunity emerged in late-May 2010, with each of the TSP stock funds dropping more than 10% from their April highs. Following this buying opportunity, the funds continued their steady recovery through the end of the year, although with some hiccups.

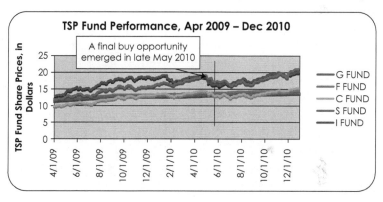

As long as the TSP stock funds remain steady or continue to increase in value, you'll want to keep adding to your G and F Funds via biweekly contributions until you have returned to at least a 20% total portfolio allocation to these funds. This might take considerable time to accomplish—up to a year or longer, assuming no further market declines—but by using your biweekly contributions to rebuild your bond fund holdings, you are allowing the stock funds time to regain most of their losses or achieve new highs while at the same time preparing for any possible further declines in the near future. An interfund transfer from the stock funds to the bond funds should be avoided during this recovery period, as this would partially offsets gains over the very long term.

By continuing to build up your bond fund holdings using biweekly or monthly contributions during this time, you will be ready to exploit future market declines in a similar fashion, as above. Using this method, however, means that the aggressive investor will experience long periods when they are not at the 70-30 allocation, which is acceptable as long as the aggressive investor continues to build a cushion with periodic contributions to the G and F Funds to take advantage of future stock fund declines.

Two sample portfolios show how using Strategy IV would have increased the aggressive investor's returns over this two-year period.

Take for example a $100,000 sample portfolio at the beginning of October 2007, invested in an aggressive allocation: $40,000 in the C Fund, $10,000 in the S Fund, $20,000 in the I Fund, and $15,000 each in the F and G Funds. An aggressive investor contributes $500 per biweekly pay period throughout these two-plus years, similarly allocated among the funds ($200 to the C Fund, $50 to the S Fund, $100 to the I Fund, and $75 each to the F and G Funds). With no reallocation during this period, the investor with this aggressive allocation would have $145,196 after the final pay period of 2010. The investor would have contributed $42,500 from early October 2007 to December 30, 2010, so that this investor's total TSP value would have stayed essentially static from October 2007. (Detailed calculations for these examples are contained in the Appendix.)

Taking this same sample portfolio using Strategy IV, had the aggressive investor conducted interfund transfers two days after each 10% decline (to account for administrative delay of conducting the transfer following the new lows), the aggressive investor would have transferred funds from the G Fund (and later from the F Fund) to the declining stock funds on eight occasions through these two-plus years: late-November, 2007; early-January, early-July, and October 2008; mid-January, February and March 2009; and late-May 2010. With approximately 1% of the total TSP value transferred to each of the stock funds on each of these occasions ($713 to each fund during the March 2009 lows; $1,194 as the funds recovered in May 2010, for example), the aggressive investor would have $151,037 on December 30, 2010. This is a difference of almost $6,000 over two years, compared to a similar allocation that does not employ Strategy IV.

The aggressive investor in this example, moreover, has not added any additional money to his TSP account or changed his biweekly allocation strategy, so that the contributions are exactly the same. Had the aggressive investor changed the 30% invested every two weeks in the bond funds and instead invested that portion into the stock funds after the 10% declines, this aggressive investor would have an even better return. And if employed over a longer time frame—10 or 20 years—Strategy IV is sure to improve returns to an even greater degree, as discussed at the beginning of this chapter.

In contrast, had an investor put 100% of his or her money ($100,000 in October 2007 and all $500 biweekly contributions) in the C Fund, he or she would have ended up with $141,622 over this same time frame. The C Fund would not yet have reached a break-even point when considering the $42,500 in contributions over this period. Similarly, with 100% invested in the I Fund, the TSP investor would have ended 2010 with $129,760, far below the break-even point.

119

Only the S Fund fared better during this period, ending 2010 with $163,486. However, the I Fund and the S Fund are both extremely volatile, and the TSP investor today does not know how these funds will perform individually in future scenarios.

Those who invested 100% into any of these funds also experienced steeper declines than either of the aggressive portfolios. The C Fund in this scenario fell to below $59,000 in late 2008, while the I and S Funds dropped to just over $54,000 each. The aggressive portfolio following Strategy IV, in contrast, fell to just over $71,000 in spring 2009 before it began to move higher. (The aggressive portfolio *without* employing Strategy IV fell to just over $75,000 in late 2008 before recovering.) While it still fell in value by a considerable amount, the aggressive portfolio did not fall as far in value compared with the 100% investments in the stock funds, and it outperformed two of three stock funds by the end of 2010 by using periodic interfund transfers following declines of 10%.

Thus, the aggressive portfolio employing Strategy IV outperformed all except one of the single stock portfolio allocations during this time frame, with relatively less volatility.

As you are no doubt aware by now, these are not hard-and-fast rules as to when to transfer money into the declining funds. When one fund has declined a full 10%, the other funds might be down only a few percentage points. You can wait for all the funds to drop below their 10% target thresholds before conducting an interfund transfer, or you can buy into the funds as soon as one of the funds dips below its 10% decline threshold. If you decide the latter, be sure to buy at even increments to keep some resources in reserve to buy into the truly steep—and ultimately more rewarding—market declines.

Nor do you have to adhere strictly to buying at 10% incremental declines. You can change your transfer threshold to every 8% decline instead of 10% target declines, which will present more buying opportunities. Conversely, you could decide to invest into the stock funds after 20% declines in any of the stock funds. This will mean, however, that you are investing relatively less often but during more significant market declines.

This strategy is, in a sense, a way to "supercharge" your Thrift Savings Plan investments. Every time one or more of the stock funds drops at least 10%, add money to it from the G Fund. While it might not feel like a "super-charge" or any sort of gain in the short term as the market declines, you will gain more over the long term by doing so.

Again, as determined in Strategy I, only those who are most comfortable with risk and with the associated gains and declines in the market should use this method. While the potential for outsized returns is great over the very long term, this strategy requires significant patience, a long-term investment horizon, and a willingness to endure sometimes steep declines in one's TSP account to be successful. The sample aggressive portfolio detailed above fell to around $71,000 using Strategy IV (compared with a fall to around $75,000 not using Strategy IV) before gradually increasing in value, for example. Those with little appetite for risk might be tempted to sell at some point during a protracted and severe decline in the markets such as took place in 2008-2009, thus realizing significant losses in their respective TSP accounts and hindering their overall investment goals. Selling stock funds during down markets should be avoided *at all costs*, and investors must be sure they can remain invested throughout the full duration of a market decline.*

It should be noted also that this Strategy is not "market timing," since it is not an attempt to pick an absolute

---

* This also means that one should refrain from taking any loans from one's TSP account. The key to maximizing long-term investment potential is to keep as much invested as possible, and any withdrawal from the TSP will detract from this strategy.

bottom in the market. Determining an absolute bottom during market declines is not the goal of this strategy. Indeed, in contrast to the market timer who tries to "predict" an absolute bottom in stock market prices and then invests a sizeable amount immediately before markets turn upward again, TSP investors employing Strategy IV simply invest at pre-determined declines in the stock funds with the understanding that any investment made at these pre-determined levels might be followed by even more declines. TSP investors, moreover, can replenish their G and F Fund bond reserves once conditions have normalized using biweekly or monthly contributions (Strategy III), instead of having to sell into a market rally to rebalance their total fund holdings. The stock funds can thus be left to grow to their maximum potential over the very long term.

Strategies I-IV have focused specifically on building wealth via the Thrift Savings Plan. Strategy V will discuss further methods outside the TSP to build even greater wealth during one's career with the government and beyond.

Summary for Strategy IV

As noted previously, Strategy IV is recommended only for TSP investors who can tolerate significant declines in their TSP accounts from time to time.

- At each 10% decline in a fund, transfer 1% of your TSP account from the G Fund to the declining fund via an interfund transfer. If other TSP funds have also declined during this time, round them up to the next highest percentage point during the transfer.

- Repeat this process if one or more of the declining funds falls an additional 10%.

- Once the declining fund or funds have recovered by 50% or to their original pre-loss levels (depending on the severity of the decline), re-build the G and F Fund holdings to at least 20% of your TSP account by allocating all of your biweekly or monthly contributions to the bond funds, as detailed in Strategy III.

STRATEGY V – BUILD FURTHER WEALTH OUTSIDE YOUR TSP INVESTMENTS

The Thrift Savings Plan is an incredibly convenient and extremely cost-effective way for U.S. Government employees and U.S. Armed Services personnel to build wealth over time. However, it is certainly not the only method by which one can build wealth over a working career. By integrating TSP investments into a holistic personal financial strategy, you can achieve truly impressive gains in wealth and, in turn, financial security, while you devote a career to Federal Government service.

Strategies I-IV dealt specifically with ways to build wealth via the TSP. Strategy V will review ways to further improve one's financial situation while continuing to invest in the TSP. This strategy focuses on three additional options: (1) paying down consumer debt; (2) saving extra funds for emergencies and other purposes in appropriate savings vehicles; and (3) investing in additional tax-advantaged vehicles, such as the Roth Individual Retirement Account (IRA) and the Health Savings Account (HSA). The final section will describe further opportunities for remaining funds, such as convenient ways to donate money to deserving charities and other efficient ways to invest extra funds.

Pay Off Consumer Debt

At first glance, paying off personal debt might seem like a strange way to build wealth outside TSP investments. After all, you can invest even while slowly paying down debt, and besides, debt is a fact of life, right? Everyone, it seems, has debts to pay each month, such as a loan for a car (or cars), credit card payments, student loan payments, home equity loan payments, and mortgage payments. And, as long as you can make the payments each month, what's the big deal?

Debt hinders the building of wealth in very direct ways. By having to make, for example, a $400 car payment each month, $300 each month to pay student loans, and another $500 to pay on maxed-out credit cards, already you have to set aside $1,200 each month before you can think about putting money in savings and investing plans, such as the TSP. With a paid-for car, you could invest that $400 a month and watch it grow over the years. The same holds for the $300 student loan payments if it was paid off, and for paid-off credit cards. Without these debts, you'd have $1,200 more each month to work with in your budget. In other words, when you can keep more of your take-home pay, you can use more to build wealth faster.

Imagine how great it would feel to have *no* debt payments each month, except perhaps a mortgage payment. If you had no debt, you would only have to pay for necessities such as rent, food, gas, utility bills, and insurance—the rest of your income would be *yours to keep*. How much more could you do with that extra money in your pocket? How much more could you contribute to your TSP accounts or save for something big like a new car, for example, if you had fewer debt payments each month? Imagine the true wealth you could build if, instead of paying the car loan companies and credit card companies and banks, you could pay *yourself* those payments each month!

Why should banks get rich and not you?

At the beginning of this book, we saw that the U.S. savings rate steadily decreased in the 1990s and early 2000s, from a rate of close to 10% to a rate hovering around zero in 2005. As a nation, we literally borrowed more than we earned. While the savings rate has improved over the subsequent years as we discovered the true dangers of excessive debt, we have a long way to go to return to a more balanced financial state.

According to the Federal Reserve, in July 2008 Americans owed $2.58 *trillion* in consumer debt. Over one-third of that amount—37%, or $970 billion—was owed on revolving credit, such as credit cards. This represented an increase of 26% since 2003.[31] According to the Federal Reserve Board's Survey of Consumer Finances in 2004, the median total debt burden (monthly interest and principal payments) for the typical American family reached 18% of income, and the percentage of those with a debt burden of 40% or more rose to over 12%. Over 46% of credit card holders—almost half— carried a balance from month to month, meaning that they failed to pay off the balances in full by the end of each billing cycle.[32] Those who fail to pay off their credit card balances are often charged double-digit interest rates, thus increasing the actual amount paid for anything charged on the card.

Young adults, moreover, are increasingly saddled with student loan debt in addition to credit card and other debt. In a column devoted to increasing debt burdens, Jonathan Clements of *The Wall Street Journal* noted that in the ten years through the 2004-2005 academic year, loans to students and parents of students increased by 194%, while the cost of four-year private and public colleges rose by only 66% and 72%, respectively. Families were taking out student loans at a faster pace than the growth in higher education costs.[33]

A separate study found that the average amount borrowed in the 2003-4 academic year for undergraduate students at a public four-year institution was $5,390, and for those attending private four-year schools, the average amount was $7,320. These amounts would exceed $21,000 and $29,000 respectively if borrowed in each year of undergraduate education.[34] The average college senior graduated in 2006 more than $19,000 in debt.[35] And many college students graduate owing hundreds or thousands of dollars on credit cards as well—all before starting their first full-time job.

When we talk about building wealth, we ought to refer to one's *entire* net worth, meaning the sum of savings and total assets, minus all debt. If you have $50,000 in your TSP and in other savings accounts, but owe $50,000 on credit cards, a car or two, and student loans, have you really built up any "wealth"? While you have saved up a tidy sum in the TSP and in savings accounts, since you owe so much to creditors, your total net worth in this scenario is actually zero.*

Consider also that, instead of *receiving* interest and dividend payments in the TSP, each of your debts is *charging you* interest—and in many cases considerable interest. With a balance of $6,000 on a credit card charging 15% interest, you will pay almost $500 *in addition to* the $6,000 original amount for the privilege of borrowing that money from the credit card company, assuming you pay off the amount in a year. That same $6,000 in a bank account collecting 5% interest would yield just over $300 in a year. The difference between owing $6,000 on a credit card and keeping that same $6,000 in your own bank account is $800 over one year. Once the

---

* Notice too that *income* is not the same as *wealth*. The news is filled with stories of high-income athletes and entertainers who make high incomes, but they have to declare bankruptcy because they spend too much. While those earning high incomes have the potential to build significant wealth, many do not take full advantage of this opportunity.

debt is paid and you no longer have to make monthly payments of $540, you can put those debt payments to work for you by contributing more to your TSP, saving for a house or car, or just saving for a rainy day in an interest-bearing savings account. After paying off those credit cards and other consumer debts for good, *you* control your own money.

Thus, by paying off your consumer debts you improve your net worth, and you can then truly concentrate on building wealth by increasing the amount you invest in the TSP and other savings plans.

There are myriad approaches to paying off debt. Library bookshelves are lined with personal finance books advocating this or that approach to managing or paying down debt. While their approaches to debt management might differ in some aspects, they all have a few concepts in common.

First, know how much you owe. List all of your total debts—the total amount you owe on each credit card, your car loan(s), your student loan(s), boat loan(s) etc.—and include your minimum monthly payment and the percentage interest rate for each debt.

Next, know how much you spend each month. Note each expense you incur for the month, starting with rent/mortgage, utilities (electricity, gas, cable, internet, and phone service), food (at home and eating/drinking out), debt payments, clothing, and entertainment and vacations. Track these expenses.

The purpose of this exercise is to determine whether your income is greater than your expenses or vice versa. It also provides you some insight as to where your hard-earned money is going. Any surprises? How much are you spending to eat out versus eating at home? Do you have any redundant expenses, such as a cell phone bill and a home phone bill? How much are you spending on clothes, shoes, entertainment, or on "weekend getaways"?

To get serious about paying off debts for good—the goal of this strategy—look for areas to cut back spending and devote that extra money each month to paying off one debt at a time. Cut back, for example, on eating out to only once a week, or not at all. Cut back on "drinking out," as well: Brew your coffee at home, and do not drink alcohol outside the house since alcoholic beverages are sold in restaurants and bars at incredible markups. Suggest alternatives when your friends or family want to go out to eat or watch a new movie, such as a potluck dinner or renting a movie. Avoid buying new clothes or planning any vacations until you have paid off your major debts. You can also look to cut back in other areas, such dropping to basic cable (or dropping cable altogether), shopping around for better car insurance perhaps with a higher deductible, or reducing cell and home phone service. Even the small reductions can add up over time, and the extra $30 or $50 each month will help to reduce debts that much more quickly.

There are differing methods of paying off various sizes of debts with the extra cash at this point. Some advisors suggest paying off your debts according to their size—paying off the smallest amounts first—and others suggest paying off your high interest-rate debts first.

Dave Ramsey is perhaps the staunchest advocate of paying off debts as quickly and aggressively as possible. In his *Financial Peace* series of books and workshops, he recommends paying off debts according to what he calls the "Debt Snowball" method. Simply order your debts from smallest to largest, and put any extra money in your budget to the lowest amount first to pay it off as quickly as possible. Once that first debt is paid off, you then apply the entire amount you had been paying toward the first debt to the second debt, in addition to the minimum payment on the second debt to pay it down more quickly. Continue this method, until all of your debts are paid off.[36]

In her book *Pay It Down!* Jean Chatzky suggests a slightly alternative method. Instead of ranking the debt from smallest to largest, she suggests ranking the debt by interest rate and paying the highest interest-rate debt first. The repayment pattern is the same as for paying down the smallest amounts first. Put any extra money towards the first debt to pay it off, and once the first debt is paid off, add that payment amount to the second debt in addition to the minimum payment on it, and so on. The debts in this method are ordered according to interest payments, not size of debt.[37]

Below is an example list of personal debts to illustrate how these two types of payment plans would work:

Debts	Amount Owed	Interest Rate
1) Car loan	$16,000	5.90%
2) Undergraduate school student loan	$5,200	4.50%
3) Graduate school student loan #2	$13,600	6.20%
4) Credit card A	$2,300	8.90%
5) Credit card B	$7,700	12.00%
6) Department store card	$700	7.50%
Total owed:	**$45,500**	

If the individual holding these debts were to pay them off from smallest to largest amount owed, she would list her debts and pay them in this order:

Low-to-High Payment Plan	Amount Owed	Interest
1) Department store card	$700	7.50%
2) Credit card A	$2,300	8.90%
3) Undergraduate school student loan	$5,200	4.50%
4) Credit card B	$7,700	12.00%
5) Graduate school student loan #2	$13,600	6.20%
6) Car loan	$16,000	5.90%

Starting with the lowest debt first, this individual would pay off the department store card debt first, and then she would apply those same monthly payments to pay off credit card A, in addition to the minimum payments already being paid monthly to credit card A. Once that was paid off, the entire monthly payment used to pay off credit card A would then go toward the next higher amount, in addition to the minimum payments already being paid, in this case the undergraduate student loan. And so forth.

If this individual were to pay off the debts based on interest rates, she would list her debts and pay them in this order:

Interest Rate Payment Plan	Amount Owed	Interest
1) Credit card B	$7,700	12.00%
2) Credit card A	$2,300	8.90%
3) Department store card	$700	7.50%
4) Graduate school student loan #2	$13,600	6.20%
5) Car loan	$16,000	5.90%
6) Undergraduate school student loan	$5,200	4.50%

In the interest rate payment plan, credit card B would be paid off first, followed by credit card A, and then the department store card. In each instance, once the previous amount was paid off, the amount going to that debt would be added to the next debt on the list, in addition to the minimum payment for that debt, and so forth until all the debts are paid off.

Logically, paying off the highest-interest-rate debts first makes sense, because the higher interest rate debts cost you more money over the long term than low-rate debts. But sometimes this means having to pay off the larger amounts first, and this might take considerable time to accomplish.

On the other hand, it is very satisfying to pay off any debt, large or small, for good. In the low-to-high pay-off example above, the individual would have paid off two debts and started paying down a third before the individual in the second example finished paying off her first major debt, credit card B. Paying off those first smaller amounts would build confidence that these debts can all be paid off in their entirety. With the smaller debts paid off quickly, the extra payments can be applied more quickly to the larger debts. Your personal situation will of course dictate which method you use.

One popular suggestion until a few years ago was to use a home equity line of credit to pay off high-interest-rate credit cards. Those who advocated this plan pointed out that a person will pay less in interest on a home loan than on the credit card payments, and the interest on this debt is tax-deductible.

However, this technique has multiple potential problems. For one, it is too easy to use the credit cards again once they are paid off to buy even more stuff. When this happens, you have to pay the extra house debt *and* the new credit card balances! Moreover, those who take out a loan against their house to pay off credit card debts can opt for a 10- or 20-year period over which to repay the loan. While they might save more on interest payments initially, the life of the loan has been greatly extended and, thus, they are less motivated to pay off the debt quickly and permanently. Finally, and most importantly, unlike credit card debts that are not secured by any of your property, the home-loan debt is now secured by your house. In other words, if you don't pay the home-loan debt, you could lose your house! Paying off debt by using more debt backed by an asset like your house is risky and should be avoided.

Incorporating Debt Payoff With TSP Investing

How would you incorporate a debt-payoff plan with biweekly TSP contributions? The simplest way is to reduce your TSP contributions while you are retiring debt (much like you are reducing expenses in other areas), using the money you would have contributed to the TSP solely for paying down debt. The faster you pay off your debts for good, the faster you can start maxing out your TSP contributions and other investment plans.

Unless you are facing a truly significant debt burden, if you are eligible for a government match on your TSP contributions, I believe that a contribution rate of between 3-5% (7-10% with the match) is appropriate, even as you pay down consumer debt. Just as it is very satisfying to pay off debts for good, it is also very satisfying to watch one's savings increase gradually as well. This also reinforces an important positive habit of saving and investing for the long term, even as you pay off outstanding debts. If you want to pay off consumer debts more quickly, a 3% contribution rate is fine, but if you want the full government match you will need to contribute 5% of your pay to the TSP. With the government match, your contributions will effectively double.

If you are not eligible for the government match, you can still contribute a few percentage points to your TSP account to get into the habit of saving, or you can simply put all the extra money you would have contributed to the TSP towards your debt pay-off plan before initiating TSP contributions. Be sure, however, to enroll in the TSP immediately after paying off the last of your debts to enjoy the benefits that the TSP offers.

Keep in mind that, by reducing your TSP contributions to pay down debt, your biweekly pay will increase as your pre-tax TSP contributions revert to after-tax income. This means that more of your income is taxed. Your post-tax income will not increase by the full amount of your pre-tax TSP contributions, as these contributions are now reduced by taxes.

No doubt about it, paying off all of one's debts can take considerable time and effort, especially for recent college graduates who perhaps have credit card balances, student loans, and car payments as well. While paying down the debts might at first feel like an agonizingly slow process in the beginning, it is well worth the effort as you watch the debts disappear once and for all and as you gain greater control over your personal finances.

Once you have paid off all of your consumer debts— and perhaps have just a mortgage left to pay—you can now increase your emergency fund and your contributions to the TSP and to other tax-advantaged vehicles, described below.

Save For Major Purchases Using Appropriate Savings Accounts

Once you have paid down your debt, use the money you had been allocating to paying off debts to increase your emergency fund to at least three or four months of expenses.

Again, make sure this savings is in an FDIC-insured account.*
There's no need to take any risk with this money; just keep
it available in an account that is quickly accessible in case
you have a real emergency. This way, if your car breaks down
and you need $2,000 to fix it, you can draw from the emer-
gency fund instead of putting it all on a credit card to be
paid off over the coming year. If you have to use your emergency fund, build it back up again for future emergencies.

Also, now that you've paid off your consumer debts,
you can increase your TSP contributions from 3-5% to
7-10%, or even up to the contribution limit for the year.
Since you've been budgeting carefully, you will not miss
this increased TSP contribution as you start to pay yourself
first instead of paying the credit card companies or banks.

Now it is time to plan for any upcoming major purchases.
Do you want to buy a house? Are you shopping for a new car,
or preparing for a big family vacation? Prioritize your next
major purchases and the time frame for each purchase. In
order to focus your savings goals, save for only one major purchase at a time. If you are planning to purchase a home, do
not plan to purchase a car or take a major vacation in that time
frame. Certainly do not do so on credit, as major purchases
on credit before purchasing a home might negatively impact
your credit score—the better your credit score (and the more
you have saved for a down-payment), the better interest rate

---

* As noted in Pre-Investment Strategy 2, FDIC stands for Federal Deposit
Insurance Corporation (FDIC) and is an insurance program that protects
savings-account holders in the unlikely event that the insured bank fails. In
2010, for example, 157 banks failed, while 140 failed in 2009 and 25 failed
in 2008. Those who had money in bank deposits insured by the FDIC were
able to get their money back up to the insured amount, even after those
banks failed.

you will receive on your mortgage.* Only after completing the purchase of a home should you consider saving for the next major purchase, such as a new or previously owned car.

Saving for major purchases can be done through a basic interest-bearing, FDIC-insured savings account. Again, nothing fancy, and these savings should *not* be in stocks or stock mutual funds, as these might decline significantly in value between the time you start saving until the time you need the money to make your purchase. Remember, the more you have available for a down-payment for a large purchase—and the more debt you have paid off—the better your interest rate will be. If you pay with cash, you will not have to worry about paying any interest (and you might be able to negotiate a better deal in the process!).

Make Payments to Yourself First

One way to prepare for a major purchase is to calculate in advance how much a monthly payment would be if you were to make the purchase today. But instead of actually making the purchase, put that hypothetical new monthly payment into a savings account each month. Try to do this pre-purchase exercise each month for a year to see whether the payments fit your budget, even during expensive occasions of the year, such as year-end holidays, summer vacations, birthdays, anniversaries, etc.

For example, you can perform this exercise ahead of buying a car. First, decide how much you plan to spend on a car. Then, determine what the payments would be for that car at a realistic percentage rate over three years. Instead of purchasing the car immediately with an actual loan, put

---

* Also consider a 15-year fixed-rate mortgage instead of a 30-year mortgage. Although your monthly payments may be higher, you'll generally get a better interest rate on a 15-year mortgage, and you'll pay off your mortgage much faster than a 30-year mortgage.

the extra monthly debt payment amount into a savings account for a year—again, to determine if these payments fit your budget throughout the year. Be sure to add an extra amount for the increased cost of insurance and property taxes, to ensure the pre-purchase exercise is realistic.

For example, you want to buy a car that costs $20,000, but you do not have the money saved up for this purchase. Monthly payments on a $20,000 loan at 8% interest over three years would come to $626.73. Add to this the cost of insurance, taxes, and maintenance—say, $75 a month for ease of calculation, although this amount will vary depending on your location—for a total of around $700 that you would be paying for this new car if you bought it now.

Instead of making the purchase immediately, save this amount each and every month over the course of a year to see if you can truly afford the payment. After a year at 2% interest, you'll have approximately $8,500 to use as a substantial down payment for this car. Incidentally, you'll find that now one-year-old $20,000 car for sale at a cheaper price. (It is a well-established fact that new cars depreciate by 20% or more within a year after leaving the new-car lot, and they depreciate another 10% or more after the second and third years of ownership). In fact, you could continue this exercise for another year and you'd most likely have enough saved up to pay cash for the now two-year-old car on the spot.

	Car Value Over Time	**Amount Saved for Car**	**Cumulative Debt Payments for New Car**
Year 1	$16,000	$8,490	($8,400)
Year 2*	$14,000	$17,153 *buy 2-year-old car @$14,000	($16,800)
Year 3	$12,000	$10,810	($25,200)

Assuming that a $20,000 car depreciates 20% in value the first year and 10% each of the next two years, the person who saves the same as a car payment for the first two years instead of buying the car on credit could purchase the now two-year-old car (assuming 30% depreciation) with cash and still have $3,153 left in savings after two years, while the person who bought the car new on a three-year payment plan would still owe thousands of dollars for the same two-year-old car. By continuing to save the equivalent of a car payment in year three (minus the amount for insurance and taxes), the person who bought the two-year-old car will have over $10,800 in savings, while the person making payments will have $0 in savings and will have paid over $25,000 for this same three-year-old car, which is now worth only around $12,000 in both cases.

By purchasing the car used after two years of saving, instead of having another year of payments—around $626 a month—you'll own the car outright with a little left over in savings. You'll be able to save another $7,500 in car payments together with the $3,100 you have left over after buying the car in the third year to use as you please.

The same pre-purchase exercise can be done before buying a house. Let's say your rent is currently $1,000 a month, and you want to buy a house that costs around $250,000. With a 10% down payment, your mortgage would be $225,000. Financed at 7.5% interest—and including a 1% property tax, basic insurance, and mortgage insurance—your monthly payment would be about $1,940 a month. As you prepare to make your purchase, put the difference between your rent and the mortgage (just over $900) in savings each month to get a feel for how your lifestyle would change after making the purchase. Of course, you would be able to deduct the interest portion of your house debt from your taxes, but you'll also want to maintain and upgrade your property, so for the purpose of this exercise, we'll say that the interest deduction and yearly maintenance costs even out.

After a few months of "pre-purchasing" the house, you should have a pretty good feel for whether or not you can afford this payment—and, at the same time, you'll be saving for your upcoming new home, too. In this example, by the end of twelve months, you'll have saved about $11,000 from the $900 each month and interest in a savings account. After another year of "pre-purchasing" the house, you'll have close to a 10% down payment for the home. You'll also have a better feel for whether you are able to afford the monthly debt payments.

Do Not Take Out a TSP Loan!

The TSP allows participants in "pay" status to borrow generally up to $50,000 through two types of loan: a general purpose loan and a residential loan. Repayment for a general purpose loan can range from one to five years, and repayment for a residential loan can range from one to fifteen years. A TSP participant in "pay" status can hold one of each of these loans at any one time. The loan must be taken from your own contributions and earnings on those contributions and cannot be taken from matching contributions.

While taking a loan from the TSP is fairly simple to do, just because you *can* take out a loan does not mean you *should* take out a loan. After all, *a loan is a loan is a loan*—instead of borrowing from a bank, you are borrowing in this case from your future growth potential of your TSP account.

A commonly held view is that, by using funds from your TSP account, you are simply borrowing from yourself and paying yourself interest on the amount borrowed. But there are three major reasons why borrowing from your TSP hinders the building of wealth.

First, you are taxed twice when repaying a TSP loan. In contrast to your initial tax-free TSP biweekly or monthly contributions, you pay back the loan with *after-tax* money, which means you *lose* between a quarter to a third of your repayment to your own TSP in the form of taxes. You are repaying each $1 loan with around $0.70 of after-tax income. And then, when you withdraw the money in your older years, the money is taxed again. Your low-interest "loan" from yourself is taxed twice—once going in, and once coming out.

Second, this loan becomes a new form of "golden handcuffs," because you are stuck in your job until you pay off your loan. Under most circumstances you are required to repay loans to your employer-sponsored retirement plans in full if you leave your job. If you do not pay the loan amount back in full, you could be charged income tax on the entire loan and a 10% penalty.

Third, you lose the benefits of potential growth. As the TSP website warns, "the earnings in your account when your loan is fully repaid are likely to be different from what your earnings would have been if you had not taken the loan," especially if you had invested in funds besides the G Fund. "Thus, even though you pay back your loan with interest, you may have less money in your account" years from now "than you would if you had not borrowed from it," according to the TSP.[38]

For example, let's say you borrowed $10,000 from your TSP to help finance the purchase of a house. After selling the shares to borrow the money, the TSP funds from which you borrowed suddenly increased by 20%. Had you left the $10,000 in your TSP, it would have been worth $12,000—you've essentially missed out on $2,000 of growth! You'll also have to use after-tax income, so that you'd have to *earn* $13,000 or more depending on your federal, state, and local tax brackets (not to mention Social Security and Medicare taxes) to pay back the original $10,000 by the time you've paid off the loan.

To avoid this, it is best to plan sufficiently ahead of time by saving for or "pre-purchasing" major items separately in an interest-bearing savings account.

Invest in a Roth IRA and other Tax-Advantaged Vehicles in Conjunction with the TSP

The Thrift Savings Plan is not the only tax-advantaged plan in which federal workers and uniformed members of the armed services can save and invest. In addition to contributing to the TSP, federal employees are also eligible to contribute to two types of Individual Retirement Accounts (IRAs)—the Traditional IRA and the Roth IRA.

In addition to the $16,500 that can be invested in the TSP, those under 50 years of age are eligible to put up to $5,000 into an IRA. Those 50 and over can put an additional $5,500 in the TSP and an additional $1,000 in an IRA as "catch-up" contributions to make up for their younger years, when they were perhaps unable to contribute as much in their tax-advantaged plans.*

The two types of IRAs differ in several important features. Contributions to a Traditional IRA are tax-deductible in the year of the contribution, up to certain income limits, while contributions to a Roth IRA—named after Delaware Senator William V. Roth, who sponsored the legislation enacting this special type of IRA—are not tax deductible and, instead, are made with after-tax dollars. While contributions to both types of IRAs grow tax-free, when money is withdrawn from the Traditional IRA account the account owner will have to pay income tax on the money that is withdrawn after the account owner turns 59½. Money withdrawn from the Roth IRA, in contrast, is tax-free.

Individual investors can deduct the amounts invested in a Traditional IRA account from his or her income taxes up to a maximum modified adjusted gross income (MAGI) limit of $66,000 for single filers and $109,000 for mar-

---

* The IRS increases these amounts from time to time, and updates can be found on the IRS website at <www.irs.gov/retirement>.

ried filers filing jointly in 2010. (These limits also gradually increase from year to year.) When this money is withdrawn after turning 59½, he or she must pay taxes on the amount withdrawn. Therefore, owners of a Traditional IRA save some on taxes initially, but have to pay taxes each year that money is withdrawn from the Traditional IRA.

Contributions to a Roth IRA are made with after-tax money and cannot be deducted the year the investment is made. But any withdrawals taken after turning 59½ are *tax free*, unlike money withdrawn from the TSP and Traditional IRAs. There are income limits for Roth IRAs, with those who are single making less than $122,000 in MAGI and those who are married making less than $179,000 able to contribute to Roth IRAs in 2011.*

Like TSP accounts, money in both the Traditional IRA and the Roth IRA can be withdrawn from the year the account owner turns 59½, without owing any penalties. The owner of a traditional IRA must begin taking minimum withdrawals by April 1 the year after turning 70½ (the IRS publishes "Required Minimum Distribution" tables that dictate the minimum withdrawal amounts). In contrast, there are no mandatory withdrawal minimums for owners of Roth IRA accounts. Roth IRA owners, therefore, can continue to keep their money in the Roth IRA and let that money grow for as long as they desire.

The Roth IRA offers one other important feature. Because you've already paid taxes on the money you contribute to the Roth IRA, you can withdraw any of that contributed money at any time without any penalty. (You will have to pay taxes and a 10% penalty on any of the gains in the

---

* Those who make more than these limits can still invest in a traditional IRA, but the amount invested is not tax-deductible, and the gains on these investments will be taxed once withdrawn after turning 59½ unless it is later converted to a Roth IRA.

Roth IRA if they are withdrawn before reaching minimum withdrawal age, however.) Thus, a Roth IRA can serve as an additional emergency savings vehicle of last resort.

For example, let's say you've invested $3,000 in a Roth IRA per year for the past five years. Over the five years the Roth IRA has grown steadily, and now the $15,000 in total investments is worth $25,000. You can withdraw the original $15,000 at any time for whatever purpose without paying any penalties, although you would forfeit any potential future gains from the withdrawn amount. You cannot withdraw the remaining $10,000 growth portion of the Roth IRA, however, without paying taxes and penalties on it.

Investing in Both the TSP and a Roth IRA

As noted earlier, you can invest in the Roth IRA even when you are contributing to the TSP. Of course, those who are just starting out or who are early in their government or military service careers are limited in how much they can contribute to either the TSP or a Roth IRA because of relatively low starting salaries. While laudable, contributing the maximum $21,500 ($16,500 to the TSP and $5,000 to a Roth IRA) on a basic government or military starting salary would be difficult indeed. This is especially true for those with young children or other financial goals. So, how can you incorporate investing into a Roth IRA account while contributing to the TSP?

One way to invest in both tax-advantaged programs is to start by contributing 5% to the TSP to get the government match. (Even if you don't get a government match, monthly contributions to the TSP allow you to participate in one of the simplest and cheapest investment vehicles in the world of personal investing.) Once any consumer debts are paid off and a cushion is set aside for an emergency fund or other major expenditures, such as a house or car, you can next contribute to a Roth IRA to take advantage of the tax-free earnings. Most investment companies that feature Roth IRA plans allow you to set up an automatic investment plan, in which you can have a specific amount withdrawn from your bank account on a biweekly, monthly, or quarterly basis.

You can also put some after-tax money from bonuses into your Roth IRA (and into your spouse's Roth IRA—he or she is also generally eligible to put up to $5,000 into a Roth IRA in addition to your own, keeping in mind income limits). Once you are able to contribute up to the maximum for a Roth IRA, increase your TSP biweekly contributions by a couple of percentage points. Each time you receive a pay increase, bump up your TSP contribution by another percentage point until you are contributing the maximum to the TSP as well.*

In this way, you are diversifying your tax obligations in your later years: Your TSP withdrawals will be taxable, while your Roth IRA contributions will be tax-free. And if you continue to work after serving with the government, you can continue to contribute to a Roth IRA in addition to any other company-sponsored plans, as long as you do not exceed the income limits.

Roth IRA investors can use the same investment strategies that they use in their TSP accounts. For example, moderate investors can keep 60% in a large-cap U.S. stock index fund and 40% in a bond index fund. Moderate investors in this example could further diversify by investing a portion in international stocks, small-cap stocks (U.S. and international), and 40% in a variety of bond index funds. Roth IRA lifecycle funds similar to the TSP's L Funds are also available.

---

* This same method can be used once the TSP implements a Roth investment option—invest 5% in the Roth TSP, then invest up to the contribution limit to a Roth IRA, and once you are comfortable with contributing these minimum amounts to both accounts, increase your TSP contributions by a percentage or two after each raise until you are contributing the maximum amount to each, taking into consideration other financial goals.

Or, Roth IRA investors can invest in alternative areas to further diversify their portfolios, since companies that offer Roth IRAs provide investors with many more investment options beyond those offered in the TSP. As noted in Strategy II, some portfolio strategists recommend investing in real estate, commodities, and international small-cap and international bond funds in addition to mainstream stock and bond index funds. Thus, more adventurous investors can include real estate and alternative investments in Roth IRA accounts along with their TSP investments to further diversify their holdings.

In all, the Roth IRA provides TSP investors with greater flexibility in diversifying both their total investment portfolio and their future tax obligations, once it is time to withdraw these funds. A Roth IRA (or non-deductible IRA for high-income workers) makes an excellent addition to any investment portfolio.

Consider an HDHP with a Health Savings Account

On December 8, 2003, President Bush signed legislation enabling the creation of tax-advantaged Health Savings Accounts (HSAs) in conjunction with High Deductible Health Plans (HDHPs). These new types of health accounts were included in legislation creating a Medicare prescription drug benefit. HSAs allow owners of these savings and investment vehicles to add money each year for future health-related expenditures. Unlike Flexible Spending Accounts (FSAs), however, contributions to HSAs do not need to be spent each year and can be kept and added to year after year for long-term growth. They are health-care versions of the TSP and IRA accounts.

HSAs must be used in conjunction with High-Deductible Health Plans (HDHPs), which are a type of health insurance plan that require owners to pay for initial medical expenses up to a certain high-deductible limit. For 2010, the IRS set the maximum upper limits at $5,950 for self-only coverage and $11,900 for family coverage, although individual health insurers often set lower limits. These upper limits are considered "deductibles," and, because they are higher than deductibles for traditional health insurance, they are called "High-Deductible" plans. Health expenses up to these maximum limits can be paid either from the HSA or out of pocket, and once the upper deductible limits are reached, the insurer covers additional costs associated with health care needs for that year as a traditional health insurer.

Because the health insurance *deductible* is higher than traditional health insurance—and individuals are required to pay more out of pocket each year for initial health care needs—the health insurance *premium* (what is paid each pay period for health insurance) is cheaper than regular health insurance. (Given the special tax considerations of the HSA, and the health insurance already provided to U.S. uniformed service members and retirees, HSAs are available only to civilian Federal Government employees who do not receive Medicare or Tricare.)

While this is a fairly new type of insurance plan, insurance providers in the Federal Employees Health Benefits Program (FEHBP) are increasingly offering HDHPs with HSAs. To sweeten the deal, up to $125 is contributed per month into participants' HSAs, although these contributions can vary from year to year depending on the size of the deductible (the higher the deductible, the more the monthly contribution offered). Those with an HDHP can contribute up to a maximum of $3,050 for individual plans and $6,150 for those with family coverage to an HSA in 2011. Those 55 and over can make catch-up contributions of $1,000. Therefore, participants can add extra to their HSA, in addition to the contributions from insurance providers, as long as total contributions do not exceed the upper limits set by the IRS. Money in HSAs can be used tax-*free* at any time for health-related expenses. After turning 65, the owner of an HSA can use the savings for non-medical expenditures as well, but withdrawals for non-medical expenses will be taxed as regular income.

Much like the TSP, savings and investments in the HSA can enjoy potentially significant growth over time. When opened at an early age, when one usually incurs fewer medical expenses, small contributions will have many decades to grow. Contributing $2,400 a year—$200 per month, some of which might be contributed by the insurance provider—from the age of 25 at a conservative 5% growth rate, will increase to over $306,000 40 years later at age 65, assuming no withdrawals were made for medical expenses over that time. The $2,400 is less than the $3,050 and $6,150 contribution limits for individuals and families, so more could be saved and used for medical expenses each year, as necessary—and the steady increase in savings over the years provides a family with an expanding cushion for medical needs over the years. Moreover, medical expenses can be paid out-of-pocket as well, to protect the tax-advantage growth in the HSA.

By increasing this initial $2,400 contribution 4% each year (just over the average inflation rate), and if it were to enjoy 8% average gains per year for 40 years, the HSA would grow to almost *$1,140,000*, assuming that health expenses over that time were paid for out of the remaining tax-deductible contributions to the HSA. These are significant sums, compared to what one would have saved tax-free before HSAs were created—that is, nothing at all. And these savings are *in addition to* savings and investments in one's TSP and Roth IRA.

Saving for future health needs is especially important, precisely because we experience more medical needs later in life. According to the Employee Benefit Research Institute, the average couple at age 65 today could need as much as $295,000 for medical-related expenses over their lifetimes. A couple living to 95 could need as much as *$550,000* to cover medical expenses![39] While the extra savings in an HSA might not cover one's entire medical needs later in life, it could provide a significant cushion and go a long way to protecting one's remaining wealth in the TSP, IRAs, real estate, and other savings. And, like these other tax-advantaged savings vehicles, any remaining funds can be passed to family members or charities of your choice upon the passing of the HSA owner.

Coupled with the monthly contributions offered by insurance providers, contributions to an HSA should be relatively simple to incorporate into a broad investment plan. As you continue to invest in your TSP (and a Roth IRA if possible), simply choose an HDHP with the accompanying HSA, and depending on automatic additions from the insurance company, start by adding $50 or $100 a month to the account—this amount is entirely tax-deductible no matter what your income might be, so your income taxes will be reduced depending on how much you contribute during the year. Your initial goal is to have enough in the HSA to cover the full deductible for the year, which can be accomplished within a year to 18 months assuming no withdrawals for healthcare needs. It will of course take longer for those who need to make withdrawals for healthcare expenses, but at least some of this savings is deposited as an added incentive to help you manage your healthcare needs.

The biweekly premium of an HDHP with HSA is less than traditional plans too, because health insurers allow participants in these plans to manage their own healthcare needs with funds from the HSA before traditional health insurance begins, thereby helping the insurance companies reduce their expenses. However, this also means that those who need more health care over several years will have to draw more from their HSAs initially to meet these greater expenses before hitting the higher yearly deductible.

The tax-advantaged savings aspect of the HSA provides a significant incentive to shop around for better deals on medical expenses. In a personal example, after our family ophthalmologist provided a prescription for new contact lenses (the eye exam was covered by the HDHP insurance), she also offered to sell a year's worth of contacts for $316. Under a traditional plan, we would have worked through the insurance company to pay for the contacts and would therefore not have considered the price of the contacts. However, the insurance company in this case offered a flat $100 to cover the contacts, with the rest coming out of our tax-deductible HSA savings. We compared the doctor's price with those quoted by an online company and a local warehouse store. The online company's price was less expensive than the doctor's quoted rate, at $256 for the year. However, the warehouse store quoted $179—plus a $30 rebate. With the rebate and the $100 provided by the insurance company, we ended up paying $49 for a year's worth of contacts, $167 less than what we would have paid at the eye doctor's office.

Similarly, after visiting a close-by but out-of-network medical office several times to have minor ailments treated, we later shopped around and found an in-network medical office that had better rates. The health clinic was a few miles farther away, but the savings more than made up for the extra travel for non-emergency treatment.

Paying more initially out-of-pocket can take some adjustment in the first year or two of having an HDHP and HSA. Most people are so used to paying small deductibles and having the insurance company pay the rest that they do not stop to consider the full costs of their healthcare needs. But the individual incentives to save and spend healthcare dollars wisely in the HDHP and HSA ultimately present a win-win-win scenario for the insurance companies, the individual worker, and for the government—which is of course financed by taxpayers. The insurance company saves money by allowing us to shop for our own basic healthcare needs. It in turn rewards us with lower insurance premiums and a tax-advantaged savings account. Because our insurance premiums are lower, the Federal Government—and ultimately, the taxpayer—also saves by having to pay a smaller amount for our health insurance benefits. What's not to love about the HDHP and HSA?

The HDHP with HSA is, as an aside, perhaps the greatest potential tool to help control healthcare costs in the United States, as it gives individuals the incentive to comparison shop for healthcare needs. This in turn increases competition and price transparency in the healthcare marketplace and that will drive down (or at least control) prices for healthcare expenditures. As individuals shop among hospitals, specialty providers, and healthcare clinics for a given procedure or service, they will demand to see, for example, the success rate and mortality rate of any given medical procedure, the training of the staff, and the itemized prices for the given procedure and for aftercare. Individual healthcare consumers will more carefully scrutinize prices to look for potential increased savings, and they will have a powerful financial incentive to undertake the necessary steps to stay healthier longer by eating healthfully, exercising, and not smoking.

And best of all, with the resources available in an HSA, healthcare consumers will not have to worry about any insurance company (or medical boards associated with any future single-payer system) saying "no" to a procedure or service: the HSA owner can in that case simply use money from his or her HSA to buy the health procedure or service outright, as long as the IRS considers it a qualified medical expense.*

Because money in an HSA might be needed to cover a medical emergency—unlike TSP or Roth IRA investments—this money should be saved and invested very conservatively. The HSA owner should probably keep an amount equal to two times the annual deductible in the savings account itself to cover any significant health issues. Once you have saved this amount, extra money can be invested in index funds, starting with a large-cap U.S. domestic fund, for example. Unfortunately, many HSA providers currently charge not insignificant fees and expense ratios—much higher than those found in the TSP or other index fund plans—that eat away at some of the growth potential. Hopefully, demand from HSA owners and increasing competition among HSA providers will drive down these fees and expenses and free up additional investment options in the near future.

What About the Rest of Your Money?

You might find yourself in the enviable position of having extra funds available even after paying all your bills in full and contributing to the TSP and other tax-advantaged savings vehicles. Or, maybe you suddenly come into money after winning the lottery or inheriting some money. If your debts are paid off in full, you are maxing out your TSP and IRA contributions, you have a significant cushion in emergency savings, and you are adequately saving for any significant purchases in the medium term, you might have some income and savings left over that you don't know what to do with.

---

* Even if the IRS denies it as a *qualified* medical expense, the HSA owner can still use that money to pay for the procedure while also paying the associated taxes and penalties for using funds from the HSA.

This is a very fortunate situation. If this is the case, you might consider sharing your good fortune by increasing contributions to your favorite charities directly or through very convenient payroll deductions via the Combined Federal Campaign (CFC). With additional funds—and if you are the fortunate recipient of a windfall of some sort—also consider investing in U.S. domestic and international stock index funds in addition to investing in tax-advantaged accounts.

Consider Increasing Charitable Contributions through the CFC

Many readers probably already contribute to one or more charities or non-profit organizations. A very convenient way to contribute even more to charities is through the CFC.

According to the Office of Personnel Management (OPM), the CFC is "the world's largest and most successful annual workplace charity campaign, with more than 300 CFC campaigns throughout the country and internationally."[40] Total contributions to the CFC have increased steadily over the past decade. In 1999, the CFC received pledges totaling over $218 million. By 2009, pledges to CFC charities had increased to over $282 million.[41]

The CFC features literally thousands of pre-screened and deserving local, national, and international charities. Ahead of open season, which takes place in the fall of each year, OPM provides a special booklet with descriptions of the thousands of charities to which one can donate. Information also includes the total amount that goes directly for charitable works and the amount used for overhead expenses, allowing donors to see at a glance how efficient each charity is at providing services.

During CFC open season, you can donate directly through CFC and you can also sign up for a payroll deduction to start the next calendar year, much like payroll contributions to the TSP. Those who donate 1% of their salary are designated "Eagle" donors, and those who donate 2% are "Double Eagle" donors. But deductions of as little as $5 each pay period are accepted, and any little amount can add up over time to make a difference over the year. A $5 periodic contribution, for example, equals $130 in donations over the year.

Every little bit helps, so consider donating to worthy causes through the CFC in addition to direct contributions during the year.

Consider Investing in Index Funds

If you still have money left over after you have all your consumer debts paid off and have an emergency fund, have maxed out your contributions to your TSP and other tax-advantaged savings plans, you have a residence and are contributing to your favorite charities, then consider investing any extra savings in basic index funds. As noted previously, index funds outperform a majority of actively managed funds and generally have expense ratios much lower than actively managed funds. They are also tax-efficient compared to regular savings and bond funds, because they are taxed at a lower capital-gains rate.

A basic allocation would be 70% in a total U.S. domestic stock index fund and 30% in an international large-cap stock index fund. You could also have a 60-40 or even 50-50 allocation and invest in small cap index funds as well, based on your investor type. It's as easy as that; there's no need to spend the hours required to research individual companies, no fear of underperforming the market, and capital gains taxes are easy to calculate.

And if you are still interested in playing the stock market by picking individual companies in which to invest, use these extra funds to do so.

Of course, money invested in stock funds and individual stocks should be money that you do not need for at least five to ten years, as these funds will increase and decrease in value just as the U.S. and international stock markets go up and down over time. Thus, be sure that you have an emergency fund to cover unexpected expenses.

Summary for Strategy V

Savings and investing do not have to be limited to the TSP, with additional vehicles available to help further enhance building and diversifying personal wealth. TSP investing should fit into an over-all personal financial plan that includes paying off debt and saving in other ways, such as in a Roth IRA and in an HSA.

- Pay off consumer debts and build up an emergency fund, equal to at least three to four months' expenses.

- Plan ahead for and use appropriate savings vehicles for major future purchases; *never* take loans from your TSP account, since this will negatively impact future account growth.

- Consider investing in additional tax-advantaged vehicles, such as a Roth IRA and an HSA in addition to the TSP.

- Contribute additional funds to non-profit charitable organizations through payroll deductions via the CFC in addition to making charitable contributions directly.

- Invest remaining savings in broad, low-cost index funds.

CONCLUSION

With the TSP and other tax-advantaged savings vehicles, Federal Government workers and their military counterparts are no longer bound by "golden handcuffs" of lifetime government service merely for retirement benefits. By maximizing savings and investing opportunities through the TSP and by using other personal finance techniques, federal workers and uniformed military personnel can choose to serve just a few years, 10 or 20 years, or an entire lifetime with the Federal Government and still enjoy opportunities to build wealth during their government service and beyond.

This book explored ways to save and invest in the TSP while also using other personal finance techniques to build personal wealth over the long term.

Pre-Investment Strategy 1 at the beginning of this book suggested building and maintaining savings for emergencies amounting to at least one month's worth of expenses starting out, and Pre-Investment Strategy 2 recommended starting out contributing 3-5% of pay to the TSP.

Strategy I helped the TSP investor establish his or her interest in and risk tolerance for investing. Strategy II, in turn, advocated allocating savings and investments among the TSP funds based on one's interest and risk tolerance, so that the TSP investor is not tempted to sell during significant declines in the market. Strategy II proposed a 50-50 allocation between TSP stock and bond funds for conservative investors, a 60-40 stock-bond fund allocation for moderate investors, and a 70-30 stock-bond fund allocation for aggressive investors, who are comfortable with potentially significant swings in their TSP total account value. For those who are simply not interested in following their TSP funds or the markets on a regular basis but who still want some potential growth in their investments over the long term, the strategy proposed investing in one of the TSP's L Funds as an alternative.

Strategy III suggested re-balancing periodically by allocating one's biweekly or monthly contributions to the underweighted TSP funds, to allow greater growth potential of TSP funds over the long term. It suggested re-balancing via interfund transfers only when TSP funds drifted more than 5% from target allocations.

For aggressive investors, Strategy IV proposed a method to "supercharge" TSP investments over time by investing into funds that drop by 10% or more. While market declines—and corresponding declines of TSP fund totals—are sometimes severe, past experience suggests that investing during these market drops can provide greater returns over the very long term.

As one continues to invest in the TSP, Strategy V suggested paying off outstanding debts for good, especially consumer debts such as credit cards and car loans. With no debt, the TSP investor has more income available with which to both invest and save for future large purchases, such as a car or house. Strategy V advocated "pre-purchasing" or saving for future purchases based on how much debt payments would be for that item for at least a year. After a year or two, money used to "pre-purchase" an item can be used as a down payment or for the outright purchase of the item. Once consumer debts are paid off, the TSP investor can increase TSP contributions and consider other savings vehicles such as a Roth IRA and an HDHP with an HSA for even more wealth-building potential.

Finally, as you build wealth, consider donating some of it to charities of your choice through the CFC and directly, as desired. Additional funds can also be invested in tax-efficient index mutual funds for long-term growth.

The building of wealth is a gradual process that takes time, effort, and patience. It requires making conscious decisions to save and invest. But over several decades you, as diligent savers and investors, should have a sizable amount of wealth available in your later years—you will have built personal *legacies* for yourselves, your families, and your favorite charities.

I wish my federal and military colleagues success in your personal journeys of saving, investing, and building wealth during your time in service and in your post-government and post-military careers.

FOR FURTHER READING

Bernstein, William. *The Intelligent Asset Allocator: How to Build Your Portfolio to Maximize Returns and Minimize Risk.* (McGraw-Hill: New York, 2000).

Bogle, John C. *Bogle on Mutual Funds.* (Dell Publishing: New York, 1994).

Chatzky, Jean. *Pay It Down! From Debt To Wealth on $10 a Day.* (Portfolio: New York, 2004).

Clason, George. *The Richest Man in Babylon.* (Signet: New York, 2004).

Malkiel, Burton. *A Random Walk Down Wall Street.* (Norton: New York, 2003).

Ramsey, Dave. *The Total Money Makeover: A Proven Plan for Financial Fitness.* (Thomas Nelson: New York, 2009).

Robin, Vicki, Joe Dominguez and Monique Tilford. *Your Money or Your Life: 9 Steps to Transforming Your Relationship with*

Money and Achieving Financial Independence. (Penguin: New York, 2008).

Siegel, Jeremy. *Stocks for the Long Run,* Fourth Edition (McGraw-Hill: New York, 2008).

Stanley, Thomas J. and William D. Danko. *The Millionaire Next Door: The Surprising Secrets of America's Wealthy.* (Taylor Trade Publishing: New York, 2010).

Stein, Ben and Phil DeMuth. *Yes You Can Time the Market!* (John Wiley & Sons: Hoboken, 2003).

APPENDIX

Investment Returns 1970-2010

If $1,000 had been invested in the equivalent to the C Fund (S&P 500 stock index fund) at the beginning of each year from 1970 to 2010, the investor's $40,000 in total contributions would have been worth over $616,000 by the end of 2010. If that same investor had invested an extra $1,000 after each 8% year-end decline in the fund—which happened a total of six times in this 40-year period—the investor's $46,000 in total contributions would have been worth over $718,000 by the end of 2010. The extra $6,000 invested following market declines yielded an extra $102,000 during this 40-year period.*

Year	Return of $1,000 Invested each Year	Return of $1,000/Year, With Extra $1,000/Year Following Decline Years
1970	$1,040.10	$1,040.10
1971	$2,332.04	$2,332.04
1972	$3,964.46	$3,964.46
1973	$4,236.67	$4,236.67
1974	$3,850.52	$4,585.82
1975	$6,654.92	$9,035.75
1976	$9,479.85	$12,428.27
1977	$9,727.40	$12,464.12
1978	$11,431.11	$14,347.37
1979	$14,723.41	$18,177.42

*   Investment returns will vary depending on the time frame and types of investments—some investments might perform better over similar future time frames, while some investments might perform worse over similar future time frames.

Year	Return of $1,000 Invested each Year	Return of $1,000/Year, With Extra $1,000/Year Following Decline Years
1980	$20,833.52	$25,410.09
1981	$20,759.31	$25,110.71
1982	$26,448.44	$31,737.57
1983	$33,640.81	$40,123.16
1984	$36,812.79	$43,701.58
1985	$49,810.79	$58,885.40
1986	$60,297.16	$71,066.00
1987	$64,515.26	$75,849.47
1988	$76,397.35	$89,614.16
1989	$101,924.57	$119,329.79
1990	$99,733.91	$116,599.57
1991	$131,427.53	$153,432.16
1992	$142,518.51	$166,199.89
1993	$157,985.17	$184,053.63
1994	$161,083.78	$187,496.34
1995	$222,994.86	$259,333.27
1996	$275,424.08	$320,105.79
1997	$368,639.15	$428,226.68
1998	$475,282.02	$551,899.66
1999	$576,491.76	$669,229.75
2000	$524,940.01	$609,238.84
2001	$463,405.74	$538,562.54
2002	$361,772.07	$421,098.22
2003	$466,851.38	$544,485.10
2004	$518,753.61	$604,833.88
2005	$545,273.51	$635,580.32
2006	$632,530.10	$737,096.36
2007	$668,310.90	$778,617.84

2008	$421,665.87	$491,159.24
2009	$534,503.26	$623,649.18
2010	$616,150.05	$718,721.34

By contributing $1,000 at the beginning of 1970 and increasing one's contribution each year by 5%, the TSP investor would have ended this 40-year period with close to $1,000,000. And by doubling a contribution after each year-end decline of 8% or more, the investor would have over $1,145,000 at the beginning of 2010. The extra $23,500 invested following market declines in total yielded an extra $150,000 during this 40-year period.*

Year	5% Increase in Contribution	Total Return	Total Return w/Add'l Investments following Declines
1970	$1,000	$1,040	$1,040
1971	$1,050	$2,389	$2,389
1972	$1,103	$4,154	$4,154
1973	$1,158	$4,533	$4,533
1974	$1,216	$4,227	$5,121
1975	$1,276	$7,551	$10,528
1976	$1,340	$11,010	$14,697
1977	$1,407	$11,526	$14,948
1978	$1,477	$13,856	$17,503
1979	$1,551	$18,249	$22,568
1980	$1,629	$26,338	$32,061
1981	$1,710	$26,668	$32,110
1982	$1,796	$34,598	$41,212

*   Investment returns will vary depending on the time frame and types of investments; some investments might perform better over similar future time frames, while some investments might perform worse over similar future time frames.

Year	5% Increase in Contribution	Total Return	Total Return w/Add'l Investments following Declines
1983	$1,886	$44,715	$52,821
1984	$1,980	$49,622	$58,237
1985	$2,079	$68,106	$79,454
1986	$2,183	$83,412	$96,878
1987	$2,292	$90,203	$104,377
1988	$2,407	$107,992	$124,520
1989	$2,527	$145,543	$167,309
1990	$2,653	$143,602	$164,693
1991	$2,786	$190,992	$218,510
1992	$2,925	$208,694	$238,308
1993	$3,072	$233,112	$265,711
1994	$3,225	$239,456	$272,486
1995	$3,386	$334,103	$379,545
1996	$3,556	$415,185	$471,061
1997	$3,733	$558,670	$633,186
1998	$3,920	$723,378	$819,191
1999	$4,116	$880,559	$996,531
2000	$4,322	$804,357	$909,775
2001	$4,538	$712,717	$809,600
2002	$4,765	$558,919	$638,102
2003	$5,003	$725,711	$834,051
2004	$5,253	$810,493	$930,620
2005	$5,516	$856,075	$982,101
2006	$5,792	$997,956	$1,143,881
2007	$6,081	$1,059,159	$1,213,095
2008	$6,385	$671,293	$768,273
2009	$6,705	$857,396	$988,515
2010	$7,040	$994,620	$1,145,486

Investment Returns of Aggressive Allocation, 2007-2010

An aggressive portfolio (70-30 Stock-Bond allocation) would have grown from $100,000 from October 2007—the peak of the stock market in the early 2000s—through the market lows of 2008 and 2009 to $148,000 in mid-January 2010 with steady contributions of $500 allocated among the funds.*

Date	C Fund	S Fund	I Fund	F Fund	G Fund	Total
1-Oct-07	$40,000.00	$10,000.00	$20,000.00	$15,000.00	$15,000.00	**$100,000.00**
11-Oct-07	$40,407.37	$10,194.09	$20,272.41	$15,062.06	$15,099.71	**$101,035.65**
25-Oct-07	$39,565.35	$9,973.79	$20,065.26	$15,345.17	$15,199.55	**$100,149.12**
8-Nov-07	$38,787.85	$9,800.65	$20,244.41	$15,420.17	$15,299.50	**$99,552.58**
23-Nov-07	$38,122.26	$9,475.20	$19,747.82	$15,639.65	$15,399.59	**$98,384.51**
6-Dec-07	$40,133.13	$10,005.57	$20,527.40	$15,741.05	$15,499.79	**$101,906.94**
20-Dec-07	$39,104.08	$9,759.99	$19,341.92	$15,869.09	$15,600.12	**$99,675.20**
3-Jan-08	$38,971.48	$9,641.63	$20,047.62	$16,077.33	$15,700.57	**$100,438.63**
17-Jan-08	$36,138.77	$8,800.64	$18,256.49	$16,326.36	$15,801.14	**$95,323.39**
31-Jan-08	$37,587.42	$9,336.22	$18,585.00	$16,401.36	$15,901.83	**$97,811.84**

* Investment returns will vary, depending on the time frame and types of investments; some investments might perform better over similar future time frames, while some investments might perform worse over similar future time frames.

Date	C Fund	S Fund	I Fund	F Fund	G Fund	Total
14-Feb-08	$37,014.91	$9,340.93	$18,233.71	$16,327.75	$15,989.74	$96,907.03
28-Feb-08	$37,773.17	$9,476.95	$19,134.01	$16,484.18	$16,090.67	$98,958.99
13-Mar-08	$36,557.90	$9,104.73	$18,744.67	$16,531.91	$16,191.73	$97,130.95
27-Mar-08	$37,076.86	$9,221.23	$18,844.67	$16,716.49	$16,279.82	$98,139.07
10-Apr-08	$38,288.27	$9,574.66	$19,430.88	$16,860.28	$16,381.12	$100,535.21
24-Apr-08	$39,281.81	$9,748.74	$19,859.50	$16,783.26	$16,482.54	$102,155.85
8-May-08	$39,780.91	$9,970.22	$20,509.98	$17,024.84	$16,570.81	$103,856.77
22-May-08	$39,930.81	$10,150.79	$20,839.76	$17,016.18	$16,672.47	$104,610.02
5-Jun-08	$40,432.93	$10,589.19	$20,683.22	$17,007.15	$16,774.26	$105,486.75
19-Jun-08	$38,912.38	$10,280.59	$19,468.50	$16,941.48	$16,876.16	$102,479.11
3-Jul-08	$36,833.59	$9,359.18	$18,713.49	$17,130.23	$16,982.10	$99,018.59
17-Jul-08	$36,986.28	$9,579.77	$18,545.16	$17,130.29	$17,082.62	$99,324.13
31-Jul-08	$37,412.28	$9,757.99	$18,668.30	$17,292.24	$17,183.38	$100,314.19
14-Aug-08	$38,417.48	$10,107.35	$18,064.23	$17,388.72	$17,284.26	$101,262.04
28-Aug-08	$38,884.60	$10,162.71	$18,108.53	$17,607.65	$17,385.25	$102,148.73
11-Sep-08	$37,585.91	$9,680.88	$16,911.97	$17,908.92	$17,485.80	$99,573.48
25-Sep-08	$36,599.30	$9,538.95	$17,278.04	$17,623.72	$17,586.18	$98,626.19
9-Oct-08	$27,775.41	$6,878.97	$12,929.30	$17,439.80	$17,686.25	$82,709.74
23-Oct-08	$27,925.42	$6,694.27	$12,416.50	$17,593.63	$17,786.01	$82,415.83

Date						
6-Nov-08	$28,055.50	$6,836.49	$12,510.38	$17,627.95	$17,886.16	**$82,916.48**
20-Nov-08	$23,563.45	$5,343.79	$10,660.61	$17,738.94	$17,987.12	**$75,293.91**
4-Dec-08	$26,699.86	$6,177.02	$11,745.24	$18,253.31	$18,086.62	**$80,962.05**
18-Dec-08	$28,190.81	$6,786.17	$13,155.02	$18,775.73	$18,180.83	**$85,088.56**
2-Jan-09	$29,931.48	$7,245.36	$13,827.69	$18,767.25	$18,276.54	**$88,048.32**
15-Jan-09	$27,327.68	$6,767.99	$12,497.13	$19,049.02	$18,365.45	**$84,007.27**
29-Jan-09	$27,584.52	$6,727.97	$12,278.46	$18,862.39	$18,455.57	**$83,908.91**
12-Feb-09	$27,516.85	$6,797.51	$12,264.27	$19,083.08	$18,548.79	**$84,210.51**
26-Feb-09	$25,048.67	$6,068.44	$11,123.36	$18,934.74	$18,643.25	**$79,818.45**
12-Mar-09	$25,218.59	$6,157.71	$11,062.68	$19,039.29	$18,738.66	**$80,216.93**
26-Mar-09	$28,183.45	$6,985.53	$12,637.41	$19,294.75	$18,834.30	**$85,935.44**
9-Apr-09	$29,236.83	$7,352.41	$13,081.29	$19,393.55	$18,928.55	**$87,992.64**
23-Apr-09	$29,289.87	$7,368.98	$13,398.08	$19,577.98	$19,021.84	**$88,656.75**
7-May-09	$31,424.78	$7,944.66	$14,582.13	$19,669.08	$19,116.24	**$92,736.89**
21-May-09	$31,018.99	$7,840.70	$15,261.78	$19,879.67	$19,212.51	**$93,213.64**
4-Jun-09	$33,136.23	$8,503.69	$15,977.76	$19,848.34	$19,309.45	**$96,775.47**
18-Jun-09	$32,524.24	$8,224.41	$15,661.72	$19,876.55	$19,408.73	**$95,695.66**
2-Jul-09	$31,972.82	$8,171.97	$15,685.88	$20,284.26	$19,508.10	**$95,623.03**
16-Jul-09	$33,780.03	$8,583.99	$16,330.79	$20,410.03	$19,607.72	**$98,712.55**

Date	C Fund	S Fund	I Fund	F Fund	G Fund	Total
30-Jul-09	$35,652.18	$9,183.71	$17,422.24	$20,567.79	$19,707.43	$102,533.36
13-Aug-09	$36,840.21	$9,607.03	$18,209.48	$20,799.24	$19,807.09	$105,263.06
27-Aug-09	$37,741.89	$9,764.27	$18,792.58	$20,984.07	$19,906.99	$107,189.80
10-Sep-09	$38,455.71	$10,051.91	$19,500.86	$21,251.05	$20,006.37	$109,265.89
24-Sep-09	$38,924.60	$10,213.37	$19,532.40	$21,393.96	$20,105.54	$110,169.85
8-Oct-09	$39,707.25	$10,445.33	$19,954.69	$21,592.37	$20,204.33	$111,903.96
22-Oct-09	$40,943.28	$10,646.91	$20,641.96	$21,617.25	$20,302.75	$114,152.14
5-Nov-09	$40,185.33	$10,234.21	$19,981.97	$21,700.36	$20,401.40	$112,503.27
19-Nov-09	$41,502.78	$10,412.93	$20,307.68	$21,980.97	$20,500.93	$114,705.30
3-Dec-09	$41,932.61	$10,484.63	$20,840.56	$22,085.54	$20,600.39	$115,943.73
17-Dec-09	$42,013.44	$10,810.79	$20,268.12	$22,186.60	$20,698.21	$115,977.16
31-Dec-09	$42,975.25	$11,145.37	$20,791.95	$22,006.02	$20,796.11	$117,714.70
14-Jan-10	$44,489.44	$11,588.34	$21,699.98	$22,302.32	$20,897.74	$120,977.83
28-Jan-10	$42,228.82	$11,086.31	$20,153.35	$22,441.90	$21,000.90	$116,911.27
11-Feb-10	$42,242.10	$11,131.87	$19,756.88	$22,488.32	$21,101.92	$116,721.10
25-Feb-10	$43,457.30	$11,607.57	$19,923.24	$22,678.34	$21,202.40	$118,868.85
11-Mar-10	$45,564.92	$12,419.49	$21,150.37	$22,804.02	$21,303.13	$123,241.93
25-Mar-10	$46,390.73	$12,537.79	$21,168.77	$22,789.92	$21,404.10	$124,291.31
8-Apr-10	$47,454.83	$12,957.37	$21,752.07	$22,901.62	$21,505.98	$126,571.87

Date						
22-Apr-10	$48,551.44	$13,534.67	$21,707.86	$23,136.91	$21,608.93	$128,539.81
6-May-10	$45,550.12	$12,505.09	$19,659.88	$23,511.68	$21,711.82	$122,938.59
20-May-10	$43,519.86	$11,923.07	$18,813.19	$23,680.01	$21,814.14	$119,750.28
3-Jun-10	$45,026.11	$12,558.49	$19,428.34	$23,641.09	$21,916.07	$122,570.11
17-Jun-10	$45,802.93	$12,666.17	$20,109.97	$23,917.29	$22,015.45	$124,511.81
1-Jul-10	$42,390.02	$11,590.91	$19,234.96	$24,209.22	$22,114.92	$119,540.02
15-Jul-10	$45,470.47	$12,306.07	$20,952.17	$24,362.03	$22,212.31	$125,303.06
29-Jul-10	$45,902.05	$12,552.99	$21,458.23	$24,525.79	$22,309.95	$126,749.02
12-Aug-10	$45,408.79	$12,186.11	$21,094.61	$24,780.42	$22,406.83	$125,876.76
26-Aug-10	$44,115.57	$11,911.32	$20,645.44	$25,065.47	$22,503.61	$124,241.41
9-Sep-10	$46,762.40	$12,673.64	$22,041.61	$24,954.36	$22,598.28	$129,030.29
23-Sep-10	$47,871.71	$12,998.23	$22,620.66	$25,210.79	$22,691.67	$131,393.05
7-Oct-10	$49,530.36	$13,629.03	$23,944.75	$25,484.94	$22,785.12	$135,374.20
21-Oct-10	$50,695.14	$13,969.81	$24,203.34	$25,524.42	$22,878.79	$137,271.51
4-Nov-10	$52,677.56	$14,734.24	$25,242.11	$25,716.16	$22,972.36	$141,342.43
18-Nov-10	$51,893.10	$14,592.04	$24,540.44	$25,441.68	$23,066.16	$139,533.43
2-Dec-10	$53,219.01	$15,212.75	$24,311.86	$25,392.34	$23,160.20	$141,296.15
16-Dec-10	$54,383.95	$15,635.44	$24,907.15	$25,120.59	$23,256.36	$143,303.49
30-Dec-10	$55,274.39	$15,999.40	$25,188.41	$25,381.35	$23,352.76	$145,196.32
13-Jan-11	$56,648.81	$16,348.69	$25,952.20	$25,602.75	$23,452.35	$148,004.79

Investment Returns of Aggressive Allocation With Interfund Transfers Following 10% Declines, 2007-2010

The same aggressive portfolio (70-30 stock-bond funds) would have grown to over $154,000 from October 2007 to mid-January 2010 by reallocating from the bond funds to the stock funds following each 10% decline in one or more of the stock funds. Bolded and italicized rows indicate an interfund transfer took place two days following a decline in a fund by 10% or more.*

Date	C Fund	S Fund	I Fund	F Fund	G Fund	Total
1-Oct-07	$40,000	$10,000	$20,000	$15,000	$15,000	**$100,000**
11-Oct-07	$40,407.37	$10,194.09	$20,272.41	$15,062.06	$15,099.71	**$101,035.65**
25-Oct-07	$39,565.35	$9,973.79	$20,065.26	$15,345.17	$15,199.55	**$100,149.12**
8-Nov-07	$38,787.85	$9,800.65	$20,244.41	$15,420.17	$15,299.50	**$99,552.58**
23-Nov-07	$38,122.26	$9,475.20	$19,747.82	$15,639.65	$15,399.59	**$98,384.51**
26-Nov-07	*$38,200.61*	*$10,290.36*	*$20,456.00*	*$15,758.43*	*$12,496.13*	*$97,201.53*
6-Dec-07	$41,175.76	$11,044.07	$21,546.48	$15,741.05	$12,581.35	**$102,088.70**
20-Dec-07	$40,114.78	$10,767.80	$20,297.19	$15,869.09	$12,676.90	**$99,725.77**
3-Jan-08	$39,973.59	$10,632.06	$21,032.80	$16,077.33	$12,772.58	**$100,488.36**

* Investment returns will vary, depending on the time frame and types of investments; some investments might perform better over similar future time frames, while some investments might perform worse over similar future time frames.

10-Jan-08	*$40,251.62*	*$11,219.71*	*$21,442.11*	*$16,104.11*	*$9,817.93*	*$98,835.49*
17-Jan-08	$37,990.83	$10,631.68	$20,069.19	$16,326.36	$9,900.92	$94,918.99
31-Jan-08	$39,503.47	$11,268.30	$20,420.40	$16,401.36	$9,992.02	$97,585.54
14-Feb-08	$38,891.58	$11,263.63	$20,024.54	$16,327.75	$10,075.13	$96,582.62
28-Feb-08	$39,678.14	$11,417.36	$21,003.44	$16,484.18	$10,166.48	$98,749.59
13-Mar-08	$38,391.49	$10,958.69	$20,566.29	$16,531.91	$10,257.94	$96,706.33
27-Mar-08	$38,926.45	$11,088.73	$20,666.29	$16,716.49	$10,341.23	$97,739.19
10-Apr-08	$40,188.32	$11,503.61	$21,299.50	$16,860.28	$10,432.94	$100,284.64
24-Apr-08	$41,221.23	$11,702.69	$21,759.72	$16,783.26	$10,524.77	$101,991.67
8-May-08	$41,735.10	$11,958.54	$22,462.87	$17,024.84	$10,608.24	$103,789.60
22-May-08	$41,882.54	$12,165.15	$22,814.53	$17,016.18	$10,700.31	$104,578.71
5-Jun-08	$42,399.43	$12,680.62	$22,633.68	$17,007.15	$10,792.50	$105,513.38
19-Jun-08	$40,795.20	$12,301.20	$21,294.98	$16,941.48	$10,884.81	$102,217.66
3-Jul-08	$38,606.15	$11,188.86	$20,459.75	$17,130.23	$10,979.76	$98,364.75
16-Jul-08	*$39,071.82*	*$12,249.75*	*$20,896.38*	*$17,175.78*	*$8,071.17*	*$97,464.90*
17-Jul-08	$39,742.96	$12,427.63	$21,253.01	$17,130.29	$8,147.01	$98,700.91
31-Jul-08	$40,185.81	$12,643.96	$21,379.52	$17,292.24	$8,234.29	$99,735.83
14-Aug-08	$41,250.70	$13,081.86	$20,673.20	$17,388.72	$8,321.69	$100,716.18

Date	C Fund	S Fund	I Fund	F Fund	G Fund	Total
28-Aug-08	$41,737.51	$13,138.80	$20,709.46	$17,607.65	$8,409.21	$101,602.62
11-Sep-08	$40,328.87	$12,501.23	$19,326.68	$17,908.92	$8,496.57	$98,562.26
25-Sep-08	$39,255.66	$12,303.38	$19,730.73	$17,623.72	$8,583.90	$97,497.40
1-Oct-08	$38,641.75	$12,617.71	$19,268.19	$17,551.93	$5,773.68	$93,853.26
8-Oct-08	$33,635.85	$11,102.87	$17,002.67	$17,544.07	$3,300.17	$82,585.62
9-Oct-08	$31,276.08	$10,330.53	$16,286.86	$17,439.80	$3,375.48	$78,708.75
23-Oct-08	$31,419.78	$10,028.07	$15,614.91	$17,593.63	$3,455.21	$78,111.60
6-Nov-08	$31,541.12	$10,216.22	$15,707.23	$17,627.95	$3,535.09	$78,627.61
20-Nov-08	$26,466.12	$7,960.86	$13,359.22	$17,738.94	$3,615.22	$69,140.37
4-Dec-08	$29,964.26	$9,177.67	$14,693.10	$18,253.31	$3,695.15	$75,783.48
18-Dec-08	$31,613.05	$10,058.44	$16,431.61	$18,775.73	$3,774.07	$80,652.90
2-Jan-09	$33,540.74	$10,714.95	$17,246.92	$18,767.25	$3,853.37	$84,123.23
15-Jan-09	$30,598.85	$9,985.03	$15,562.62	$19,049.02	$3,931.30	$79,126.82
16-Jan-09	$31,627.73	$10,873.44	$16,446.14	$19,005.51	$1,546.58	$79,499.41
29-Jan-09	$31,653.09	$10,679.36	$16,036.11	$18,862.39	$1,622.76	$78,853.71
12-Feb-09	$31,545.94	$10,760.38	$15,986.98	$19,083.08	$1,699.36	$79,075.75
24-Feb-09	$29,982.38	$10,584.55	$15,393.34	$16,724.66	$1,700.89	$74,385.81
26-Feb-09	$29,411.82	$10,297.27	$15,199.04	$16,714.52	$1,776.14	$73,398.79
11-Mar-09	$28,934.03	$10,580.60	$15,425.29	$14,586.29	$1,777.95	$71,304.16

Date						
12-Mar-09	$30,318.75	$11,162.83	$15,805.47	$14,674.54	$1,853.09	$73,814.67
26-Mar-09	$33,842.76	$12,622.86	$18,012.45	$14,888.63	$1,930.13	$81,296.84
9-Apr-09	$35,067.50	$13,245.48	$18,602.60	$14,982.00	$2,007.10	$83,904.69
23-Apr-09	$35,091.23	$13,235.25	$19,010.88	$15,141.54	$2,084.04	$84,562.94
7-May-09	$37,609.38	$14,229.40	$20,649.08	$15,228.98	$2,161.16	$89,878.01
21-May-09	$37,084.37	$14,003.65	$21,569.89	$15,408.96	$2,238.57	$90,305.45
4-Jun-09	$39,576.51	$15,148.46	$22,540.47	$15,401.55	$2,316.13	$94,983.11
18-Jun-09	$38,806.70	$14,611.89	$22,053.55	$15,440.24	$2,394.04	$93,306.42
2-Jul-09	$38,110.13	$14,479.89	$22,046.75	$15,773.69	$2,472.04	$92,882.51
16-Jul-09	$40,225.85	$15,171.35	$22,912.63	$15,888.17	$2,550.16	$96,748.16
30-Jul-09	$42,417.08	$16,192.93	$24,403.67	$16,027.60	$2,628.38	$101,669.65
13-Aug-09	$43,792.59	$16,901.18	$25,466.30	$16,224.52	$2,706.67	$105,091.25
27-Aug-09	$44,826.68	$17,139.84	$26,241.92	$16,385.19	$2,785.07	$107,378.70
10-Sep-09	$45,636.96	$17,606.98	$27,191.32	$16,610.09	$2,863.48	$109,908.83
24-Sep-09	$46,156.05	$17,852.21	$27,195.86	$16,738.17	$2,941.94	$110,884.23
8-Oct-09	$47,046.96	$18,220.27	$27,744.60	$16,909.72	$3,020.42	$112,941.97
22-Oct-09	$48,474.49	$18,534.67	$28,661.13	$16,945.47	$3,098.92	$115,714.68
5-Nov-09	$47,540.33	$17,779.19	$27,705.90	$17,026.83	$3,177.53	$113,229.78
19-Nov-09	$49,062.31	$18,052.80	$28,118.85	$17,263.16	$3,256.35	$115,753.48

Date	C Fund	S Fund	I Fund	F Fund	G Fund	Total
3-Dec-09	$49,534.00	$18,140.43	$28,818.23	$17,361.38	$3,335.24	$117,189.28
17-Dec-09	$49,593.23	$18,668.23	$27,988.39	$17,456.87	$3,413.93	$117,120.64
31-Dec-09	$50,692.47	$19,209.64	$28,673.67	$17,330.77	$3,492.71	$119,399.27
14-Jan-10	$52,442.66	$19,936.96	$29,887.99	$17,580.06	$3,572.18	$123,419.86
28-Jan-10	$49,742.16	$19,037.22	$27,720.04	$17,705.96	$3,651.99	$117,857.38
11-Feb-10	$49,722.22	$19,079.60	$27,137.18	$17,758.42	$3,731.52	$117,428.93
25-Feb-10	$51,117.19	$19,859.24	$27,328.32	$17,924.25	$3,811.02	$120,040.02
11-Mar-10	$53,561.05	$21,212.80	$28,974.39	$18,039.30	$3,890.65	$125,678.19
25-Mar-10	$54,496.69	$21,379.45	$28,962.59	$18,043.81	$3,970.39	$126,852.94
8-Apr-10	$55,711.77	$22,059.66	$29,723.83	$18,147.87	$4,050.38	$129,693.51
22-Apr-10	$56,964.38	$23,007.37	$29,626.77	$18,349.89	$4,130.64	$132,079.07
6-May-10	$53,408.35	$21,222.22	$26,795.23	$18,662.64	$4,210.97	$124,299.41
20-May-10	$50,993.32	$20,199.63	$25,604.95	$18,811.72	$4,291.27	$119,900.89
26-May-10	$52,023.69	$21,555.86	$26,336.60	$18,783.00	$711.27	$119,410.41
3-Jun-10	$53,957.80	$22,484.18	$27,655.44	$18,796.22	$786.76	$123,680.40
17-Jun-10	$54,849.03	$22,637.44	$28,583.36	$19,031.19	$862.64	$125,963.66
1-Jul-10	$50,722.57	$20,676.34	$27,297.52	$19,278.80	$938.60	$118,913.82
15-Jul-10	$54,369.24	$21,912.88	$29,692.61	$19,415.76	$1,014.55	$126,405.03

29-Jul-10	$54,846.14	$22,313.53	$30,368.06	$19,561.50	$1,090.58	$128,179.81
12-Aug-10	$54,217.80	$21,622.51	$29,811.94	$19,779.77	$1,166.65	$126,598.66
26-Aug-10	$52,634.90	$21,096.21	$29,135.82	$20,022.44	$1,242.79	$124,132.15
9-Sep-10	$55,754.25	$22,407.79	$31,065.04	$19,948.77	$1,318.87	$130,494.72
23-Sep-10	$57,038.40	$22,943.29	$31,840.20	$20,168.80	$1,394.95	$133,385.64
7-Oct-10	$58,976.37	$24,018.47	$33,663.20	$20,403.13	$1,471.08	$138,532.24
21-Oct-10	$60,325.13	$24,580.90	$33,986.16	$20,449.69	$1,547.29	$140,889.18
4-Nov-10	$62,646.14	$25,888.00	$35,404.37	$20,618.22	$1,623.54	$146,180.27
18-Nov-10	$61,675.38	$25,600.30	$34,379.96	$20,413.03	$1,699.87	$143,768.54
2-Dec-10	$63,213.53	$26,651.56	$34,019.63	$20,388.26	$1,776.27	$146,049.26
16-Dec-10	$64,559.69	$27,354.49	$34,812.68	$20,184.84	$1,852.90	$148,764.61
30-Dec-10	$65,579.32	$27,953.77	$35,166.04	$20,409.10	$1,929.60	$151,037.84
13-Jan-11	$67,172.69	$28,526.68	$36,192.76	$20,601.82	$2,006.63	$154,500.59

ENDNOTE REFERENCES

1. Havemann, Judith. "Federal Workers Are Facing Fundamental Pension Choice; New Plan May Loosen 'Golden Handcuffs,'" in *The Washington Post,* 20 July 1987: A01.
2. Causey, Mike. "The Federal Diary," in *The Washington Post,* 2 November 1988: D02.
3. Causey, Mike. "A Super-Thrift Plan," in *The Washington Post,* 23 February 1989: D02.
4. Middleton, Timothy. "A Government Retirement Plan That Gets It Right." 1 March 2005. Accessed 21 March 2011 in <moneycentral.msn.com/content/Specials/P110681.asp>.
5. Watson Wyatt Worldwide. "Thrift Savings Plan Participant Survey Results 2006-2007." November 2007: 12, 16. Accessed 8 March 2011 in <www.frtib.gov/pdf/FOIA/2006-TSP-Survey-Results.pdf>.
6. The President's Commission to Strengthen Social Security. "Strengthening Social Security and Creating Personal Wealth For All Americans." 21 December 2001: 7-8. Accessed 10 October 2008 in <www.csss.gov/reports/Final_report.pdf>.

7. Sessions, Jeff. "A Bipartisan Fix for Retirees," in *The Washington Post*, 26 December 2006: A25.

8. Weller, Christian E. and Shana Jenkins. "The 401(k) Fee Effect: The Costs of 401(k) Accounts Are Eating Into Americans' Retirement Returns. What Should Be Done?" in *Financial Planning*, 1 May 2007: 1.

9. *Berkshire Hathaway Inc., 2004 Shareholder Letter.* p 4. Accessed 8 March 2011 in <www.berkshirehathaway. com/2004ar/2004ar.pdf>.

10. *Berkshire Hathaway Inc., 2006 Shareholder Letter.* p 21. Accessed 8 March 2011 in <www.berkshirehathaway. com/letters/2006ltr.pdf>.

11. Loomis, Carol. "Buffett's Big Bet." 9 June 2008. Accessed 8 March 2011 in <money.cnn.com/2008/06/04/news/ newsmakers/buffett_bet.fortune/>.

12. Malkiel, Burton. *A Random Walk Down Wall Street.* (New York: Norton, 2003), p 357.

13. French, Kenneth R. "The Cost of Active Investing," in *Journal of Finance*, Vol 63 Iss 4, August 2008. Accessed 8 March 2011 in <ssrn.com/abstract=1105775>.

14. Clements, Jonathan. "Parting Shot: What I Learned From Writing 1,008 Columns," in *The Wall Street Journal*, 9 April 2008: D1.

15. Barr, Stephen. "Thrift Savings Plan Opens Up to Members of Uniformed Services," in *The Washington Post*, 8 October 2001: B02; "In Effort to Recruit, Military to Begin Offering Matching Contributions to TSP Participants," in *The Washington Post* 11 January 11: B02; "Benefits," U.S. Army website. Accessed 10 October 2008, in <www.goarmy.com/benefits/after_the_army.jsp>.

16. Siegel, Jeremy. *Stocks for the Long Run.* 4th ed. (New York: McGraw-Hill, 2008), p 13.

17. Siegel, Jeremy. *Stocks for the Long Run.* 4th ed. (New York: McGraw-Hill, 2008), p 13.

18. "Remarks by Chairman Alan Greenspan At the Annual Dinner and Francis Boyer Lecture of The American Enterprise Institute for Public Policy Research, Washington, D.C." 5 December 1996. Accessed 8 October 2008, in <www.federalreserve.gov/boarddocs/speeches/1996/19961205.htm>.

19. *Berkshire Hathaway Inc., 1999 Shareholder Letter.* p 3. Accessed 8 March 2011, in <www.berkshirehathaway.com/letters/1999htm.html>.

20. Buffett, Warren and Carol Loomis. "Mr. Buffett on the Stock Market," in *Fortune Magazine,* 22 November 1999. Accessed 8 March 2011, in <money.cnn.com/magazines/fortune/fortune_archive/1999/11/22/269071/index.htm>.

21. Buffett, Warren. "Buy American. I Am," in *The New York Times,* 16 October 2008. Accessed 8 March 2011, in <www.nytimes.com/2008/10/17/opinion/17buffett.html?dbk>.

22. Federal Retirement Thrift Investment Board. "Participant Behavior and Demographics: Analysis for 2000-2005." Accessed 8 March 2011, in <http://www.frtib.gov/pdf/FOIA/Behavior_Demographics_Final.pdf>.

23. Watson Wyatt Worldwide. "Thrift Savings Plan Participant Survey Results 2006-2007," November 2007: 29. Accessed 8 March 2011, in <www.frtib.gov/pdf/FOIA/2006-TSP-Survey-Results.pdf>; Barr, Stephen. "Thrift Savings Plan Growing and Changing," in *The Washington Post,* 8 January 2008: D04.

24. Causey, Mike. "More Feds Join Club Millionaire!!!" Federal News Radio, 7 January 2011. Accessed 8 March 2011, in <www.federalnewsradio.com/?nid=20&sid=2223107>.

25. Watson Wyatt Worldwide. "Thrift Savings Plan Participant Survey Results 2006-2007," November 2007: 7-9, in <www.frtib.gov/pdf/FOIA/2006-TSP-Survey-Results.pdf>.

26. Newell, Elizabeth. "TSP Participation Among Service Members Up, But Overall Percentage Rate Dips." GovernmentExecutive.com 19 July 2010. Accessed 8 March 2011, in <www.govexec.com/dailyfed/0710/071910e1.htm?oref=rellink>.

27. Stanley, Thomas J. and William D. Danko. *The Millionaire Next Door: The Surprising Secrets of America's Wealthy.* (New York: RosettaBooks, LLC, 2010), p 100.

28. Lynch, Peter. *Beating the Street.* (New York: Simon & Schuster, 1994), p 33.

29. *Berkshire Hathaway Inc., 1997 Annual Report.* Accessed 8 March 2011, in < http://www.berkshirehathaway.com/letters/1997.html>.

30. *Berkshire Hathaway Inc., 2004 Annual Report:* p 4. Accessed 8 March 2011, in <www.berkshirehathaway.com/2004ar/2004ar.pdf>.

31. Federal Reserve Statistical Release. "Consumer Credit." 8 September 2008. Accessed 8 October 2008, in <www.federalreserve.gov/releases/G19/Current/>.

32. Bucks, Brian K., Arthur B. Kennickell and Kevin B. Moore. "Recent Changes in U.S. Family Finances: Evidence from the 2001 and 2004 Survey of Consumer Finances," in *Federal Reserve Board's Survey of Consumer Finances 2004*: A33-34. Accessed 8 October 2008, in <www.federalreserve.gov/PUBS/oss/oss2/2004/bull0206.pdf>.

33. Clements, Jonathan. "The Debt Bubble Threatens to Derail Many Baby Boomers' Retirement," in *The Wall Street Journal* 6 March 2006: D1.

34. College Board. *Trends in Student Aid 2007*: p 13. Accessed 8 March 2011, in <www.collegeboard.com/prod_downloads/about/news_info/trends/trends_aid_07.pdf>.

35. Block, Sandra. "In Debt Before You Start," in *USA Today*, 12 June 2006. Accessed 8 March 2011, in <www.usatoday.com/money/perfi/college/2006-06-11-debt-cover-usat_x.htm>.

36. Ramsey, Dave. *Financial Peace Revisited.* (New York: Viking, 2003), pp 89-92.

37. Chatzky, Jean. *Pay It Down! From Debt To Wealth on $10 a Day.* (New York: Portfolio, 2004), pp 159-170.

38. See TSP website, "TSP Loan Program," in <www.tsp.gov/features/chapter11.html>.

39. Fronstin, Paul. "Savings Needed to Fund Health Insurance and Health Care Expenses in Retirement," Employee Benefit Research Institute, Issue Brief No. 295, July 2006. Accessed 8 March 2011, in <www.ebri.org/pdf/briefspdf/EBRI_IB_07-20061.pdf>.

40. Office of Personnel Management website <www.opm.gov/cfc/index.asp>.

41. Office of Personnel Management website. "Combined Federal Campaign: Campaign Results, Trends and History." Accessed 12 December 2010, in <www.opm.gov/cfc/Results/index.asp>.

ABOUT THE AUTHOR

W. Lee Radcliffe is a former U.S. Army Reservist who earned a bachelor's degree at the University of Kansas and a master's degree in international policy studies at the Monterey Institute of International Studies. He began his civilian career in the Federal Government in the summer of 2001. Since that time he has researched the history of the TSP and different investing methods, and after testing a range of strategies using data from past bull and bear markets, he devised his preferred TSP investing strategies. During this same period he talked with many co-workers who were taking remarkably different approaches to investing in the TSP and found that others had the similar questions about investing in the TSP. He wrote this book to give newer TSP investors ideas on how to invest in their personal TSP accounts and how these methods can fit in with their personal financial goals. In short, he wrote the book he wishes had been available when he was first starting out investing in the TSP.

Made in the USA
San Bernardino, CA
21 November 2012